A Pictorial Guide to West Virginia's Civil War Sites

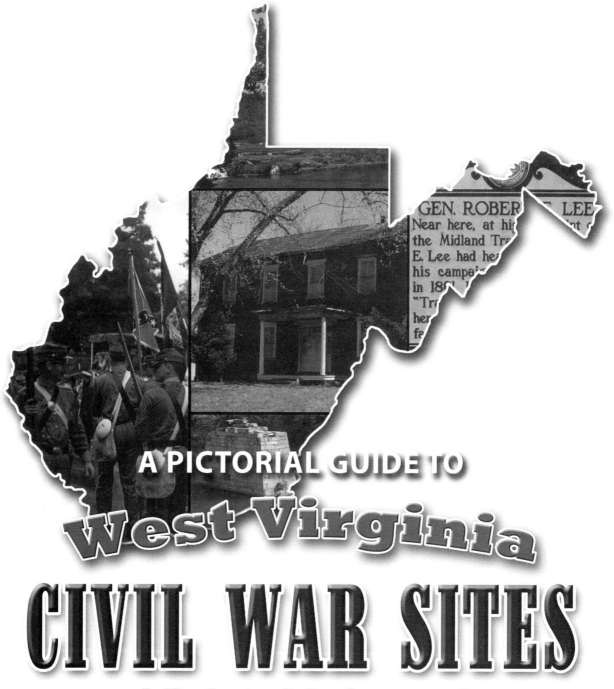

GEN. ROBER... LEE

Near here, at hig...
the Midland Tr...
E. Lee had he...
his campa...
in 18...
"Tr...
he...
fa...

A PICTORIAL GUIDE TO
West Virginia
CIVIL WAR SITES
and Related Information

STAN COHEN

quarrier
press

Charleston, West Virginia

14   13   12   11   10   9   8

Printed in the United States of America

Library of Congress Control Number: 90-60031
ISBN-13: 978-1-891852-26-8
ISBN: 1-891852-26-4

Book & cover design: Mark S. Phillips

Distributed by:

West Virginia Book Company
1125 Central Avenue
Charleston, WV 25302
www.wvbookco.com

Introduction

West Virginia, or Western Virginia as it was known at the opening of hostilities in 1861, was, after Fort Sumter, the first area of the nation to feel the effects of actual open warfare. The area that became, in June of 1863, the new state of West Virginia, played a major role in the Civil War, one that was altogether unique among the states of the so-called "borderland" that separated the territory of the Federal Union and the Confederate States and was claimed, and fought over, by both. It was the soil and people of West Virginia that witnessed the first campaigns, the first "battles," and the emergence of military personalities who would rise to the upper heights of prominence on both sides of the conflict. Although the war in West Virginia continued to be fought until hostilities ended in the Spring of 1865, after those first campaigns our conflict was largely overshadowed by more momentous events in the larger eastern and western theaters.

For West Virginia, the war began at Harpers Ferry, at what is now the state's easternmost point. On April 18, 1861, only five days after South Carolina fired on Fort Sumter and only one day after the Richmond Convention passed the Virginia Ordinance of Secession, the Virginia Militia under Maj. Gen. Kenton Harper occupied Harpers Ferry. The referendum that voted Virginia out of the Union took place on May 23 (with 34 western counties sending in no returns) and on June 3, at Philippi, occurred the first so-called "land battle" of the war. In a significant incident leading up to this engagement, on the day prior to the state-wide referendum (May 22), Thornsberry Bailey Brown of Grafton became the first Federal battle casualty of the war. He was killed at the Fetterman Skirmish, just outside of Grafton, as the two forces maneuvered toward Philippi. At the Battle of Philippi, sometimes referred to as "The Philippi Races," Union forces under Col. (later Brig. Gen.) Benjamin Kelley routed the Confederate forces of Col. George Porterfield, and chased them through the town with its famous covered bridge. This action was but the prelude to further, more serious campaigns where Union forces, under overall command of Gen. George B. McClellan, engaged Confederates at Belington, Rich Mountain (McClellan's great victory) and Corrick's Ford (near present-day Parsons, in Tucker County). It was the Rich Mountain (July 11, 1861) victory that brought

General McClellan national attention and brought about his elevation to the overall command of the eastern Union armies. It was the action at Corrick's Ford that saw the fall of the first general officer on either side of the struggle, when Confederate Brig. Gen. Robert S. Garnett fell mortally wounded while leading a rear-guard action.

Almost simultaneously came the vital Kanawha Campaign, fought for control of the important central Kanawha Valley with its turnpike that ran over the mountains, down to Lewisburg and beyond, and eventually to Richmond, the Confederate capitol far in the distance. Indeed, Robert E. Lee, in the first days of the conflict, called the Kanawha Valley "a dagger pointed at the heart of the Confederacy." Early action in the Kanawha Valley resulted in the important Battle of Scary Creek (July 17, 1861) which, though a Confederate victory, actually had the effect of forcing the southern troops, under the command of Gen. (former governor) Henry A. Wise to evacuate the Kanawha Valley as far as Gauley Bridge. After Wise was more or less superseded by Gen. John B. Floyd (a former U.S. War Secretary) as Confederate commander, he attempted a thrust at the Federal forces based near Gauley Bridge. This action resulted in the Battle of Carnifex Ferry (Sept. 10, 1861), one of the larger engagements fought on West Virginia soil. The resulting Union victory ended (except for intermittent raiding) any Confederate hopes of regaining the Kanawha Valley.

For the next four years of the war West Virginia was, for the most part, an armed camp, with "bushwhackers" and partisan rangers (or "guerrillas" as we would call them today) abounding, and scattered small campaigns being fought back and forth across the rugged landscape. Of greater significance, is that the 34 (eventually 52) counties constituting what was then known as Western Virginia, through a series of mass meetings and conventions (especially the two Wheeling conventions) "seceded from secession" and formed the 35th state of the United States: West Virginia.

West Virginia, even after the finalization of statehood on June 20, 1863, was a place of conflicting loyalties, to the Federal government on the one hand and the mother state of Virginia and the Confederacy on the other. There was never anything like a unity of opinion regarding loyalties or any of the political questions and consequences flowing from those loyalties. Because of the deep divisions among its people and also, in part, because of its location as a border area, West Virginia remained a battleground and, in many locations, conquered and occupied territory until the end of hostilities. From within the borders of what is now West Virginia, approximately 29,000 young men, at one time or another, were enrolled in the Federal service, while an estimated 16-18,000 (it is harder to be precise when dealing with Confederate records) fought under "the Stars and Bars." While a fair group of those on Federal rolls saw service as "home guards" nearly all of those in the Confederate forces fought on bloodstained battlegrounds. Many who enlisted from what is now the Mountain State became parts of famous Virginia units that did not "make their parole" until after the final capitulation of the Army of Northern Virginia.

The land of West Virginia itself was intensely fought over. According to historian Boyd Stutler, there were 632 encounters within the present state borders that can be categorized as battles, skirmishes, engagements, raids, actions, etc. Some, like Philippi, Scary, Carnifex Ferry, or Corrick's Ford, while trivial by standards soon to be set in other theaters, because of their occurrence early in hostilities, caught the attention of the nation. Others, such as Droop Mountain (November 1863), though employing large numbers of troops on both sides and having major significance to state developments, were scarcely noted by the public at large. Shortly after the close of hostilities, in 1867, Grafton, West Virginia, became one of the earlier established national cemeteries, containing primarily, several hundred Union dead from the state.

The Civil War, in one form or another, raged within our borders for the entire four years of the great fraternal conflict, and there is not an area or even county in the state that does not have some claim to some action, activity, or a direct relationship to events or people associated with those events. The war was, and remains, the single most cataclysmic event to ever occur in West Virginia, and it is the great historic watershed that not only gave the state birth but laid the foundation for nearly everything and everyone that came after.

— **Michael J. Pauley**

Purposes of this Book

This book has two main purposes. First, it is a guidebook to the most important as well as some little-known sites that have a connection with the Civil War in West Virginia. I have provided a general description of the location of each site for those who wish to actually visit them, but I would strongly urge that a good state roadmap and a copy of *West Virginia Atlas and Gazetteer* be carried along for more precise directions. Of course local inquiry will be needed for some, and a few are very difficult to visit without a guide, precise directions or permission from the local land owner.

The second purpose of the book is to provide the casual reader with a better understanding of the events that occurred in the state during the momentous years of the Civil War through a description of sites that played a role in the conflict. This volume could well be a continuation of my first Civil War book, *The Civil War in West Virginia, A Pictorial History*, first published in 1976. In any case, I hope this volume will whet the appetite of those who want to learn more about the events that shaped the history of West Virginia.

Many of these sites are private residences or private property and I would strongly urge the reader to respect this. Others, such as the battlefield state parks, cemeteries and monuments are, of course, open to the public. I would welcome comments from readers as to corrections or omissions for future reprints. I have tried to find sites in all parts of the state in as much as the entire state was affected by the conflict. Some areas, particularly along major turnpikes, rivers or populated areas, naturally had more sites to describe. In traveling around the state doing research for this book, I was amazed to see how much is still intact and marked from a period of history that ended 150 years ago. It was also surprising to discover that most of the Civil War monuments and graves that I found were from the Confederate side—in a Union state!

It would be virtually impossible to include every house or building in the state that was standing at the time of the war or every cemetery that contains Civil War graves, but residents of the state might consider documenting any local historic sites that are not already marked.

To all of you who read this book—Happy Historical Hunting.

— **Stan B. Cohen**

A Note on This Edition

This revised edition commemorates the sesquicentennial of the Civil War.

Since my first printing in 1990 there has been continued interest in the sites and many changes and new organizations to help preserve and restore them.

To name a few, the Rich Mountain Battlefield Foundation has done a great job preserving several of the major battles of the war. Fort Mullegen in Petersburg has been preserved to one of the best sites in the state. The Civil War Trails Association has placed signs throughout the state. A great new museum has opened in the Cultural Center in Charleston with a great emphasis on the war. A large display on the formation of the state is now in Independence Hall in Wheeling. The largest private Confederate collection, The Rosanna A. Blake Confederate Collection is now housed at Marshall University. Parkersburg has upgraded their Fort Boreman Park and other groups in several counties have formed to preserve and interpret sites in their areas.

In addition many new private and government books and brochures have been published to give a new perspective on the history of the war in West Virginia. In general, although war is a terrible situation and hard to understand, it is a fact of our life and heritage and the events and individuals that participated should not be forgotten.

— **Stan B. Cohen**

Acknowledgments

This book project could not have been completed without the assistance of my good friends and fellow historians: Michael J. Pauley, former historian with the Historic Preservation Unit in Charleston who co-authored with me *Historic Sites of West Virginia*; Tim McKinney of Kanawha Falls, author of *The Civil War in Fayette County, West Virginia*; Terry Lowry of South Charleston, who has authored three books, *The Battle of Scary Creek, September Blood* and *The 22nd Virginia Infantry Regiment*; and Jack Dickinson of Barboursville, author of several West Virginia Civil War books. They provided editorial comments and corrections and suggested additional sites and photographs. Bill Wintz, of St. Albans, also an author of West Virginia Civil War books, provided photos and information on the Kanawha Valley.

In addition, much help was furnished by Joe Ferrell, of St. Albans, who provided photos and information on Civil War generals and Congressional Medal of Honor recipients buried in the state; Dave Gilbert, of Winchester, Va., who provided photos in Jefferson County; Bill McNeel, of Marlinton, editor of *The Pocahontas Times*, who added photos and information on Pocahontas County; and Richard Andre, of Charleston, co-author with me on three book projects, who made many trips to photograph sites. I also wish to thank Gary Gibson, Gary Bays, Jody Mays, Bob Skeen, and Paul Marshall as well as Rod Collins, formerly of the Historic Preservation Unit; Fred Armstrong and Debra Basham of the West Virginia State Archives; Noble Wyatt, of "Little Round Top* in Kanawha County; Dr. Robert Conte, historian of The Greenbrier Resort; Gordon Simmons, who provided the photos from Wood County; and Michael Fahrion, of Fairview Park, Ohio, who provided the information on his great-great-grandfather, Lewis Fahrion; and the hundreds of people throughout the state who have provided information, photographs and directions over the past 14 years of continuing research on this project.

A big thanks to my editor, Jackie McGiffert, and to Leslie Over, officer manager of Pictorial Histories.

Most of the photographs in this book were taken by the author or furnished by the Historic Preservation Unit. I have acknowledged the contributors of other pictures. I have tried to provide at least one photo of each site where possible, but some were just not accessible or available. I also have included new discoveries of Civil War photos taken in West Virginia just prior to, during or shortly after the war. Photographs of wartime activities in the state are fairly rare for several reasons including terrain features, the small number of troops involved and the mainly guerrilla or partisan nature of the conflict. Some new maps, broadsides and paper memorabilia are also included for general interest.

Sites marked by an asterisk (*) are listed on the National Register of Historic Places.

THE NEW STATE.

The Counties Comprising the New Commonwealth of West Virginia, the Thirty-Fifth State of the Union.

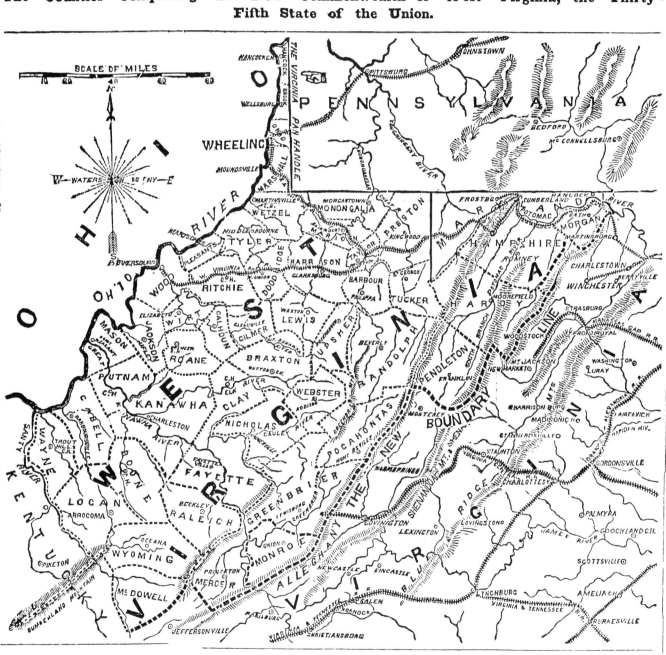

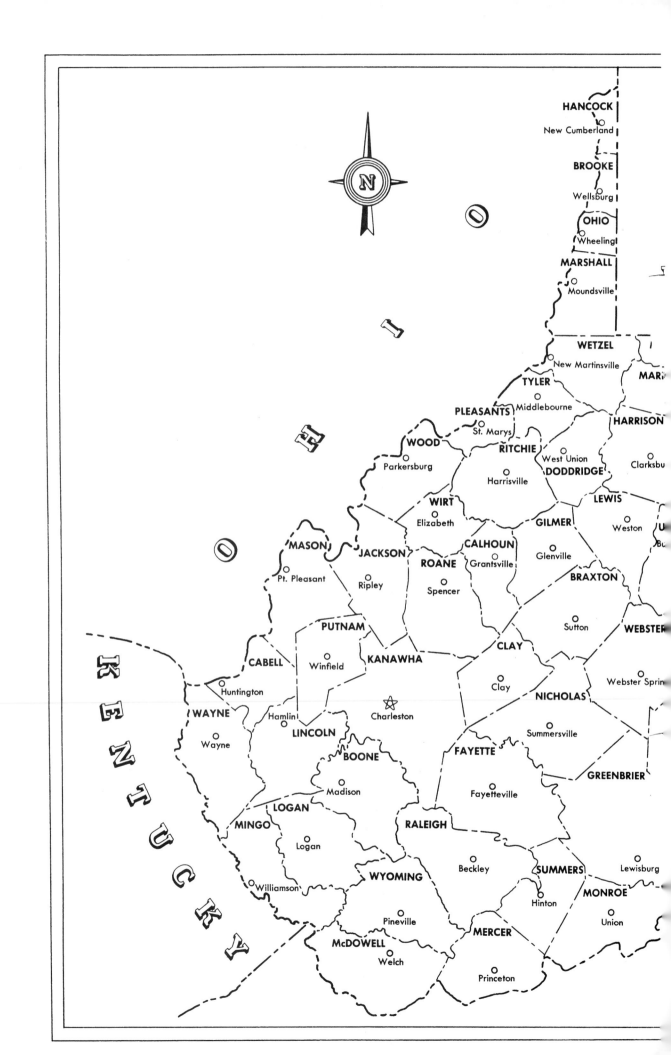

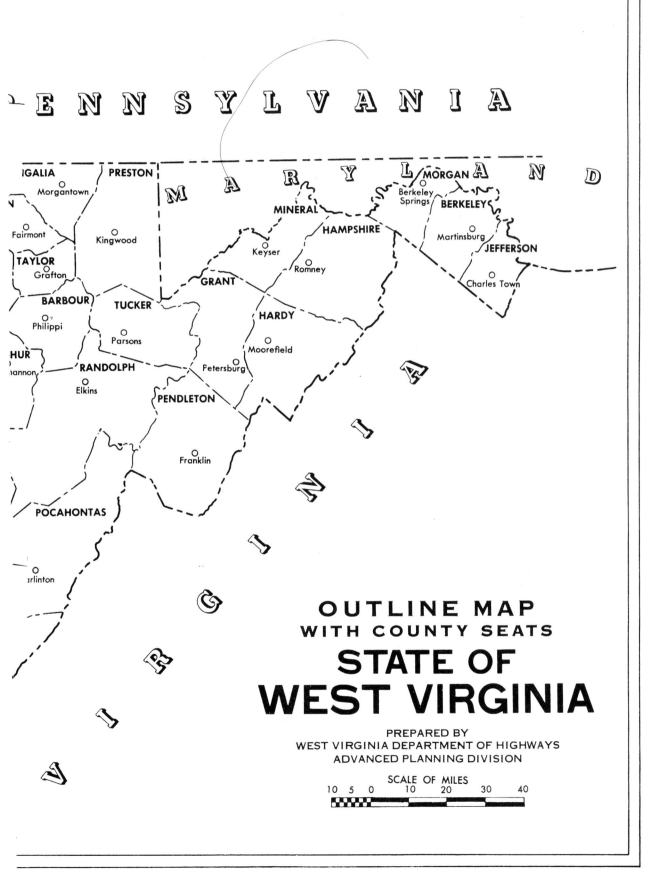

PENNSYLVANIA

MARYLAND

VIRGINIA

IGALIA
PRESTON
Morgantown
MINERAL
MORGAN
Berkeley
Springs
BERKELEY

Fairmont
Kingwood
HAMPSHIRE
Keyser
Martinsburg

TAYLOR
Grafton
Romney
JEFFERSON

GRANT
Charles Town

BARBOUR
TUCKER
HARDY
Philippi
Moorefield
Parsons

HUR
RANDOLPH
Petersburg
hannon
Elkins
PENDLETON

Franklin

POCAHONTAS

arlinton

OUTLINE MAP
WITH COUNTY SEATS
STATE OF
WEST VIRGINIA

PREPARED BY
WEST VIRGINIA DEPARTMENT OF HIGHWAYS
ADVANCED PLANNING DIVISION

SCALE OF MILES

10 5 0   10   20   30   40

THE NEW STATE,

The Division of the Old Dominion and the Appearance of a New Star.

Size and Population of West Virginia,
&c.,   &c.,   &c.

We present to-day an accurately drawn map of the new State which is about to be erected from that portion of the Old Dominion which lies west of the Alleghany Mountains, and to be called WEST VIRGINIA. The new Commonwealth, as will be seen, will embrace forty eight counties, of which McDowell, Mercer, Monroe, Greenbrier and Pocahontas form the southeastern tier; and down to the southern line of these counties, including all the islands in the Ohio river. It will contain about twenty-four thousand square miles, and a population, according to the United States census of 1860, numbering three hundred and fifty thousand six hundred, of which only a little more than twelve thousand seven hundred are slaves.

The bill which has just passed the House of Representatives, recognizing the new State government, passed the Senate at the last session, but was not taken up in the House until within a few days of adjournment—too late to secure at that time any final action upon it. It gives the new State three members of Congress, and provides for the gradual emancipation of slavery, by declaring that all children born of slave parents within its limits after the 4th of March, 1863, shall be free from their birth, and that all slaves now within the State under ten years of age shall become free at the age of twenty five; and further, that no slave shall be permitted to come into the State for permanent residence.

The eastern and western sections of Virginia have been gradually drifting apart for a number of years. The people of the two divisions have very little feeling in common so far as State government is concerned, and their interests have always been in opposite directions. Those of the western portion have long contemplated a movement of this kind, contending that they were unjustly taxed for the support of Southern chivalry, and to keep up the aristocratic ideas and practices of the "first families" of the eastern section; but they were held back by the fear that constitutional objections would overpower any propositions for the erection of a new State. When the rebellion broke out, however, they saw an opening through which they might bring their desired object before Congress with reasonable chances of success, and their loyalty to the government was not the least of their arguments in presenting their claims.

In 1861 they formed a provisional government, which was recognized by Congress, elected a Governor and other State officers and framed a constitution, which was presented to the people, and by them adopted by a vote of over a hundred in favor to one against.

Nothing now remains but the President's sanction to the bill to reduce the proportions of the Old Dominion a little over one-fifth, and add another star to the Union galaxy.

The officers of the provisional government are—

Governor—Francis H. Pierpoint.
Lieutenant Governor—Daniel Paulsley.
Attorney General—James S. Wheat.

The State as it now stands is represented in the United States Senate by Whitman T. Willey, who is the author of the bill for the admission of the State, and John S. Carlile, who has been accused of entertaining secession proclivities, and in consequence has been requested to resign his seat by the provisional State Senate. There are also three members of Congress from that section in the House of Representatives, representing the First, Tenth and Eleventh districts. Their names are Joseph E. Segar, William G. Brown and J. B. Blair.

After the bill becomes a law by the signature of the President, of course an election will be ordered to fill the positions now held by the provisional officers, and for such others as have been created by the new constitution.

The following table gives the names of the counties composing the proposed new State, together with the slave and total population of each:—

County.	Slaves.	Total.
Hancock	2	4,445
Brooke	18	5,494
Ohio	165	22,422
Marshall	29	12,997
Wetzell	16	6,703
Marion	63	12,722
Monongahela	101	13,048
Preston	67	13,312
Taylor	112	7,463
Tyler	18	6,517
Pleasants	15	2,945
Ritchie	38	6,847
Doddridge	34	5,203
Harrison	582	13,790
Wood	176	11,046
Jackson	55	8,306
Wirt	23	3,751
Roane	72	5,381
Calhoun	9	2,562
Gilmer	52	3,759
Barbour	95	8,958
Tucker	20	1,428
Lewis	230	7,999
Braxton	104	4,992
Upshur	212	7,292
Randolph	183	4,990
Mason	376	9,173
Putnam	580	6,301
Kanawha	2,184	16,150
Clay	21	1,787
Nicholas	154	4,627
Cabell	305	8,020
Wayne	142	6,747
Boone	156	4,840
Logan	148	4,938
Wyoming	64	2,861
Mercer	352	6,819
McDowell	—	1,535
Webster	3	1,555
Pocahontas	252	3,958
Fayette	271	5,997
Raleigh	57	3,367
Greenbrier	1,525	12,211
Monroe	1,114	10,757
Pendleton	244	6,164
Hardy	1,073	9,864
Hampshire	1,213	13,913
Morgan	94	3,732
Total	**12,754**	**350,599**

The News of the Passage of the Bill in Wheeling.

[From the Wheeling Intelligencer, Dec. 11.]

The news of the passage of the bill through the national House of Representatives for the admission of the new State of West Virginia was received with demonstrations of approval all over the city. We received the special despatch announcing the glorious news about three o'clock in the afternoon, and by four o'clock it was spread throughout the city. Everywhere there was a jubilant feeling. The news was read in the hall of the House of Delegates just as that body adjourned, and was received with three cheers. The new State men are congratulating each other in all directions upon the successful delivery of the new born infant to whose coming they have looked for such a long period and with so much solicitation. It is indeed a subject for joyful congratulation. It brings with it equal taxation, equal representation, industry, power, developed resources and a realization of all the ardent hopes which have animated the breast of all true Western Virginians for many long years. It tells of a happy release from merciless taskmasters, from conspiracy and rebellion, from injustice and oppression, and all the innumerable wrongs which Western Virginia has suffered so long and so patiently.

Last evening an old babymaker captured by Gen. Kelley at Romney was brought out, and a salute of thirty-five guns was fired in honor of the new state.

"Glory to God in the highest!" West Virginia has been admitted into the Union of States. The thirty-fifth star has been added to the constellation. The consummation so devoutly wished for has at last been reached. At last we are rewarded for all our labors, and have reached that happy haven where our works do follow after.

People of West Virginia, at last your toil is requited. All your sacrifices, all your devotion, all your patience and suffering, is at last worthily repaid. How the heart swells with grateful emotion to the Divinity that shapes our ends, rough hew them how we will.

Now, fellow citizens, one and all, the die is cast, and let us have no more divisions between us on this question. Let us be of one mind, and have such a jubilation over this grand triumph as the occasion demands. Let us rejoice over the day of our deliverance. In every town, far and near, at every schoolhouse, at every cross road, at every place where people do congregate, let a mass meeting be held. Bring out your speakers, bring out your babymakers if you have any, bring out your music, run up your flags, and let there be such a grand and universal rejoicing as the Western Virginia hills never saw before.

People of Wheeling, you who have gained so much by this success, shall we not have such a demonstration here as will be worthy our ancient name and fame? Throw out your banners this morning. To-night, we suggest, let the people assemble at some place suitable, where there will be room enough, to hear some of the numerous excellent speakers who are in the city and will be present. There are a dozen elegant speakers in the Legislature, in addition to others in the city, who will address the people. Their hearts are now overflowing. Give them a chance. Let us have a display of fireworks too, not surpassed by that of last Fourth of July. Let the houses be illuminated as our hearts are, and let the whole city be vocal with our joy.

What say you? shall we not? And if so, let us move early this morning and set the thing going. It may be thought better to take more time to get ready for a suitable demonstration. We hope a meeting of the citizens will be held to-day to consult about it.

CONSTITUENT CONVENTION OF VIRGINIA, ASSEMBLED IN THE CUSTOM-HOUSE AT WHEELING, OHIO CO., JUNE, 1861.

Table of Contents

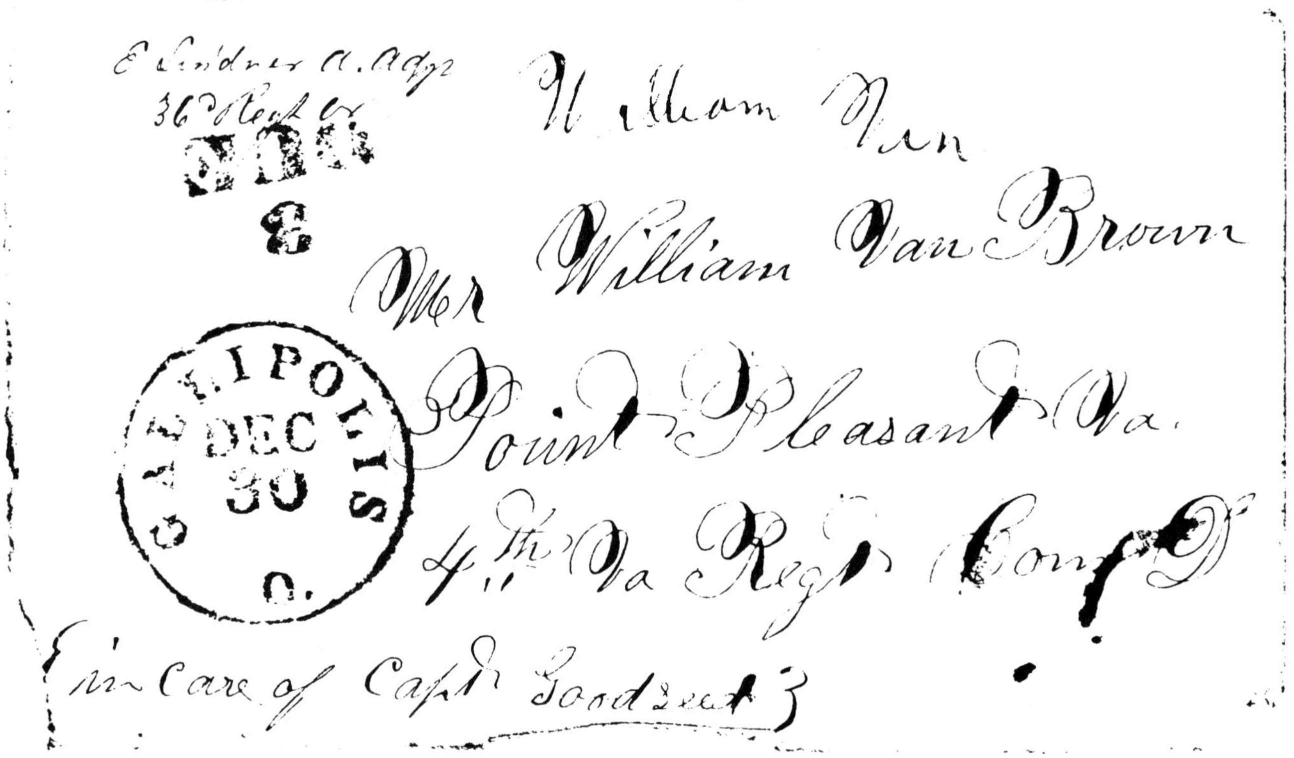

E Sandner A. Adjt
36 Regt O.
PAID
3

Mr

William Van

William Van Brown

Point Pleasant Va.

4th Va Regt Confd

GALLIPOLIS
DEC
30
O.

{ in Care of Capt Goodrect }

xiv

Barbour County

View of **Belington** in the distance from the Laurel Hill Battlefield site. Confederate Camp Laurel Hill is to the left (arrow) now the site of the city's water supply. On July 10, 1861, Gen. George B. McClellan, advancing quickly, left an artillery unit to bombard the Confederate camp as he hurried his main force southward against the Confederates on Rich Mountain. Gen. Robert S. Garnett, in command at Laurel Hill, was deceived by the ruse and did not discover until too late that he had been outflanked. Garnett retreated to the east and north to Tucker County. The Rich Mountain defenders were routed and fell back to Laurel Hill. There they found the camp abandoned, and 555 troops surrendered to the Federals.

Remnants of the **Parkersburg and Staunton Turnpike** can still be traveled on Laurel Hill In 1823, the Virginia General Assembly ordered surveys to be made for a road to extend from Staunton, Virginia, over the Alleghenies and across western Virginia to the junction of the Little Kanawha and Ohio rivers at Parkersburg. It was not completed until 1847 due to financial difficulties and the necessity of changing the route to avoid natural barriers. The road had an immediate and far-reaching effect on the development of this part of West Virginia and was a major transportation artery for both sides during the war.

Confederate Trenches in Belington.

Camp Laurel Hill, east of Belington on the old Parkersburg and Staunton Turnpike. Now the site of the city's water supply.

ARMY HEADQUARTERS
—1861—
This village was held by Colonel George Porterfield until he was relieved of command by General Robert Garnett, (C.S.A.). In 1861, it became the headquarters of Generals George McClellan and J. J. Reynolds of the Union Army.

Graves of Civil War soldiers on a hill above Camp Laurel Hill, near Belington, Barbour County.

Civil War Park and Plaques, at the west entrance of the covered bridge in Philippi, Barbour County.

Lewis Fahrion, sergeant Battery B, 1st O.V.L.A. Photo taken in Cleveland, Ohio, April 20, 1861.

The First Shot

Lewis Fahrion was born in Esslingen, Germany on July 30, 1843. He and his family emigrated to America in 1852. They first came to Medina, Ohio, where Lewis' uncle had established a successful farm. Friedrich, Lewis' father, died in 1855. Shortly thereafter the family moved to Cleveland, Ohio. Lewis became a railroad engineer, and joined the Cleveland Light Artillery, a local militia unit.

When hostilities exploded in Charleston Harbor, Lewis and the rest of the light artillery promptly answered Lincoln's first call to arms. The unit left Cleveland on April 21, 1861. The guns were immediately rushed to the "front" at Marietta, Ohio, where they were to defend the river crossing from the Rebels.

When McClellan decided to move against the Confederates in western Virginia, troops were sent from Wheeling and Marietta. Lewis' gun was one of the two guns of the Cleveland Light Artillery that were chosen to accompany the troops. They moved across the country by rail to Grafton. From there an attack was launched against the Confederates concentrated at Philippi. When the order to open fire was given, Lewis was the first to pull the lanyard and fired the first shot of the Battle of Philippi.

In those early days of the war the Cleveland Light Artillery fought in several other battles in West Virginia including Laurel Hill and Corrick's Ford. Nearing the end of their three-month enlistment, the unit was sent back to Columbus where on July 25 Lewis was discharged.

In September 1861 the artillery was reorganized and designated the 1st Ohio Volunteer Light Artillery. Each of the original six-gun crews formed the core for a six-gun battery. Lewis was promoted to corporal of Battery "B" and later to sergeant. With the 1st O.V.L.A. Lewis fought in the Western Theater under General Rosecrans where he was engaged in several battles including Mill Springs, Ky., Perryville, Ky., Lavergne, Tenn. and Stones River, Tenn. His last battle was at Chickamauga where the battery was heavily engaged on both days of the fight. On the last day Lewis' battery was in the center of the Union line and involved in hand-to-hand combat during the day. At one point Confederate artillery was so close that the batteries exchanged canister fire. The battery withdrew about 5:00 p.m. having exhausted its ammunition after firing 1,145 rounds.

Sometime during the afternoon of the second day of the battle Lewis was wounded in the leg. He did not rejoin the battery until November. While he was recuperating, the battery fought at Chattanooga. This was the last battle for Battery B, 1st O.V.L.A., and they were put in reserve for the rest of the war.

At the end of the war the unit was sent back to Columbus, Ohio, where Lewis was discharged from the service in July 1865.

Lewis returned to Cleveland and resumed his career as a railroad engineer. He married Clara Hechler and had two children. In 1872 they moved to Delaware, Ohio; then in 1889 Lewis bought 100 acres of land near Pickens in Randolph Co., W.Va. He built a farm there and moved his family to the mountains that he fell in love with during his Civil War service. He died in 1932.

Site of the **First Shot** of the first land battle of the Civil War on College (Battle) Hill on the campus of Alderson-Broaddus College, just north of Philippi on U.S. Route 250.

Covered Bridge over the Tygart Valley River at Philippi. Until it burned in February 1989, the bridge was the longest two-lane covered bridge still in use on a Federal highway. It was rebuilt to the original design in 1991. Erected in 1852 by Lemuel Chenoweth, it served both sides during the war. Reputedly Chenoweth won the construction contract by placing a model of the bridge between the seats of two chairs and walking its length. The astonished members of the Board of Public Works immediately awarded him the contract.

Hanger Plaque on Walnut Street at the Crim Memorial Church, Philippi.

Hanger Plaque at the Philippi Baptist Church across from the courthouse.

On June 3, 1961, a **re-enactment** was held in the streets of Philippi, 100 years after the Battle of Philippi or as it's sometimes called, the "Philippi Races."

Battle of Philippi, June 3, 1861. In the foreground, Federal artillery firing from College (also known as Battle, Talbott and Broaddus) Hill. Federal forces are entering the town on the left, Confederate tents and cavalry are in the center, and in the distance Federal and Confederate troops are firing at each other. *Leslies Illustrated Weekly*

Federals driving the Confederates from the town of Philippi. The courthouse is to the left.

Berkeley County

The **Flick House,** on the site of the present Berkeley County Library, was built in 1803. During the war a Federal officer, searching the house for Confederate spies, rode his horse through the wide hall, up the circular staircase, and over the polished floors in defiance of the Confederate sympathizer who owned it.

***Boydville,** 601 South Queen Street in Martinsburg. It was built in 1800 by Gen. Elisha Boyd and was the home of General Boyd's son-in-law, Charles James Faulkner I, minister to France in 1860-61, and his son, Charles James Faulkner II, a U.S. senator from 1887-99. During the war, Capt. F.G. Martindale, an officer of the First New York Cavalry in command of Federal troops, was ordered to destroy the house and issued orders that Mrs. Faulkner, family and servants vacate within an hour. Mrs. Faulkner saved her home by appealing to President Lincoln. The President's message read:

> *"The property of Charles James Faulkner is exempt from the order of General David Hunter for the burning of residences of three prominent citizens of the Shenandoah Valley in retaliation for the burning of Governor Bradford's house in Maryland by the Confederate forces."*
>
> *Dated: July 18, 1864*
> *Signed: Abraham Lincoln*

***B&O Station** (old hotel), East Martin and North Water streets in Martinsburg, was built in 1849 and survived the burning of the railroad shops by Gen. Stonewall Jackson on June 20, 1861.

* *Sites marked by an asterisk are listed on the National Register of Historic Places.*

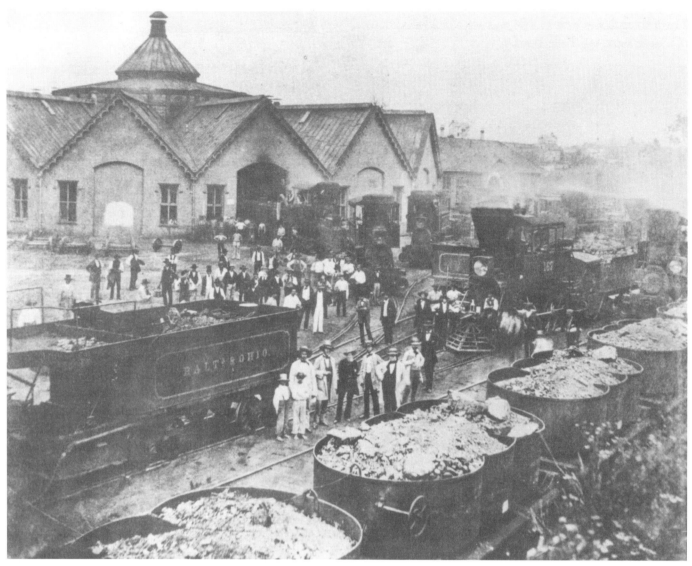

The Baltimore and Ohio roundhouse at Martinsburg in 1860. Several Winaus "Camelback" engines and three-pot gondolas are shown. Much railroad equipment and shop machinery was removed from here in 1861 and sent south. *Baltimore & Ohio Railroad Museum*

*Railroad Roundhouses** across from the B&O station. These roundhouses were built in 1866 and 1872 to replace the ones destroyed by Confederates on June 20, 1861. The 1872 building was destroyed by fire in 1990, but has since been restored.

*Berkeley County Courthouse at the northwest corner of King and Queen streets in Martinsburg. Built in 1856, the building was occupied by Federal troops who destroyed many of the county records. Belle Boyd, famous Confederate spy, was imprisoned in this building several times in 1863. The building was modernized to its present look in 1908.

Benjamin Reed Boyd House, 126 East Race Street in Martinsburg. It was built in 1854 and was a childhood home of Confederate spy Belle Boyd.

Belle Boyd site, on the corner of South and South Queen streets in Martinsburg.

Belle Boyd's childhood homesite, on the corner of Spring and East Burke streets in Martinsburg.

*Greenhill Cemetery, 486 East Burke Street in Martinsburg. The cemetery was patterned after one in Paris by David Hunter Strother and surveyor I.P. Kearfott in 1854. It is an outdoor museum of stone-carvers' art and Victorian symbolism. Among those buried are Strother, Capt. E.G. Albiertis, who commanded the Berkeley Company at Harpers Ferry during John Brown's raid, 30 unknown Confederate soldiers, and W.H. Hick, who sponsored the constitutional amendment that gave the vote to ex-Confederates in West Virginia after the war.

Norborn Hall, 396-398 West Race Street in Martinsburg. Home of David Hunter Strother (1816-88) a well-known artist, author and soldier. Under the name of Porte Crayon, he illustrated magazines and wrote for *Harpers New Monthly Magazine.* During the war he obtained the rank of brevet brigadier general in the Federal army and was chief of staff to his cousin, Gen. David Hunter.

Grave of David Hunter Strother, better known by his pen name, Porte Crayon.

*Van Metre Stone Arch Bridge, on Old Warm Springs Road on county Route 36, three miles east of Martinsburg. This three-arched stone bridge crosses Opequon Creek. It was erected in 1832 and is the second oldest bridge in the state. The bridge was frequently used by both armies. It was built by the same builder and is almost identical to the famed "Burnside Bridge" at Antietam.

Pettigrew Monument, 200 yards west of Edgewood Manor on U.S. 11 at Bunker Hill. The granite column has an Ionic capital topped by four stacked cannonballs. Brig. Gen. James Johnston Pettigrew of North Carolina was a Confederate leader in the assault on Cemetery Ridge during the Battle of Gettysburg. During the retreat southward after the battle, the general was fatally wounded in Maryland on July 19, 1863 and died at Edgewood Manor.

*Bunker Hill Presbyterian Church at Bunker Hill. It was built in 1854 and used as a stable. It was heavily damaged during the war. The building just behind the church, now used as a gym, was the Methodist church during the war.

*Edgewood Manor, on U.S. 11, one-half mile north of the intersection at Bunker Hill. This beautiful brick home was built in 1838 by Gen. Elisha Boyd on land which was part of a former Fairfax grant. Brig. Gen. James Petigrew died here in July 1863.

1st Battle of Falling Waters, 1861. Col. Thomas J. Jackson was promoted to brigadier general due to his actions at the First Battle of Falling Waters. This was before he became "Stonewall" at First Manassas. The first cavalry engagement of the war took place at this battle. It was also the first battle for Confederates T.J. Jackson and J.E.B. Stuart. The first cannon shot in the Shenandoah Valley was also fired here.

Mt. Zion Church, Hedgesville.

*Morgan Chapel and Cemetery** on state Route 26, 0.2 miles west of the intersection of U.S. Route 11, Bunker Hill. This 1851 brick church, surrounded by a cemetery that contains the grave of West Virginia's first white settler, Morgan Morgan, (1688-1766), was severely damaged by artillery in the war; the patching is still very discernible. The most interesting aspect, however, is the interior of the church, which contains extensive graffiti on the walls, pencilled there by soldiers from both sides when the church was being used as a hospital during the war.

Ruins of the B&O Railroad's Colonnade Bridge in Martinsburg, Berkeley County. It was destroyed by Stonewall Jackson's troops on June 13, 1861. The site is now occupied by the East Burke Street underpass in downtown Martinsburg.

Stonewall Jackson Monument, just south of junction of U.S. 11 and Springs Mills Road, Berkeley County. The monument is inscribed: "In Memory of General 'Stonewall' Jackson.

"This tablet is erected by the Berkeley County Chapter, United Daughters of the Confederacy, to commemorate an instance of the General Jackson's remarkable bravery at all times in face of the greatest danger.

"On this site, July 2, 1861, General Jackson was seated under an oak tree, giving orders, when fired upon by Federal troops. A cannon ball cut off a limb of the tree, but Jackson unhurt, rode calmly away."

Falling Waters, four miles southwest of Williamsport, Maryland, on U.S. 11 and I-81, is the site of the **2nd Battle of Falling Waters** on July 14, 1863. Gen. Robert E. Lee's army, retreating from Gettysburg, was attacked by Federal forces under Gen. George C. Meade, but succeeded in crossing the Potomac River. As the Confederates fell back from Gettysburg, they found that the Potomac was swollen with heavy rains and that the bridges both here and at Williamsport had been destroyed by the enemy. The forward detachments of Lees army reached the river on July 5 and for days there were cavalry skirmishes between the two armies. On July 6 a Federal corps launched a heavy attack, and on July 9 Lee arrived with the bulk of his army. Impatient at the slow progress being made in rebuilding the bridge, he ordered the warehouses along the C&O Canal to be torn down and their timbers used to construct pontoon bridges. Meade timidly delayed his attack from day to day, but finally advanced in force on July 14, only to find that under cover of darkness Lee and his forces had crossed the river at several places and retreated south.

The Porterfield/Crockett House on the Valley Turnpike (U.S. 11) was the site of the heaviest fighting. The grandfather of Davy Crockett built the log home which is now covered by siding.

Naylor Memorial Hall is a Civil War Era church in Hedgesville.

*Hedgesville, on state Route 9, six miles northwest of Martinsburg. This historic village had much Civil War activity with armies passing back and forth many times. Many of the houses, buildings and churches in the area are of pre-Civil War vintage.

Braxton County

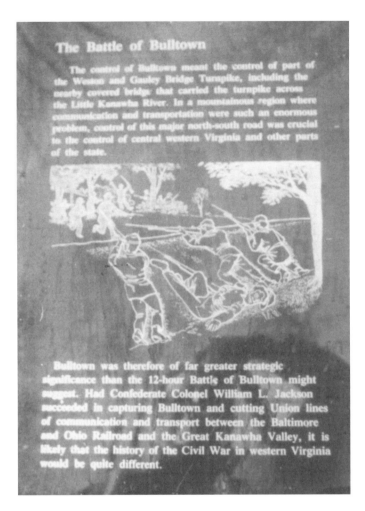

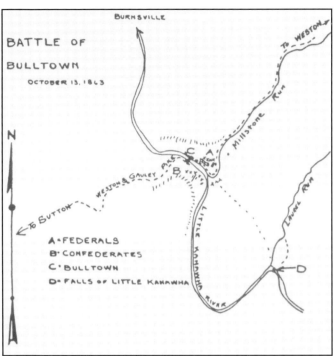

Map of the Battle of Bulltown. Reprinted from Roy Bird Cook, "The Battle of Bulltown," *West Virginia Review* 9 (1938):255.

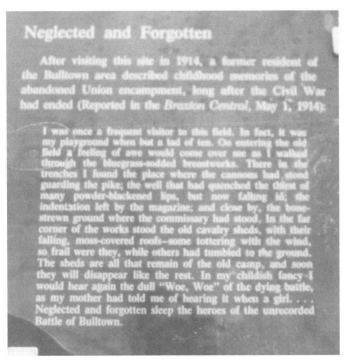

*__Bulltown Historical Area,__ just off U.S. 19 on the Millstone Run Road near Bulltown on Burnsville Lake. This was the site of a Federal fort that guarded the covered bridge across the Little Kanawha River on the route of the Weston and Gauley Bridge Turnpike. This 110-mile turnpike, completed in 1858, connected central western Virginia at Weston in Lewis County to the falls of the Great Kanawha River at Gauley Bridge in Fayette County. The bridge was a very strategic site for control of the road. A Confederate force under the command of Col. (later Brig. Gen.) William L. "Mudwall" Jackson, a first cousin of Stonewall Jackson, attacked the Federal force under Capt. William Mattingly at 4:30 a.m. on Oct. 13, 1863. The surprise attack was foiled when an over-enthusiastic southern officer shouted, "Charge!" The cry alerted the Federal troops and after a 12-hour battle the Confederates were repulsed. Eight Confederates were killed and five wounded; one Federal was killed and two wounded. One civilian, Moses Cunningham, who lived at the bottom of the Federal fort, reportedly stepped from his farmhouse, hollered "Hurrah for Jeff Davis," and was nipped by a Federal bullet. Threatened but not executed, he reportedly said: "Hark the tomb, a doleful sound, my ears attend the cries; ye living man come view the ground where you damn Yankees must shortly die."

Federal trenches on the hill overlooking the Little Kanawha River.

View of the **Cunningham House, McCauley Barn** and **U.S. Corps of Engineers Interpretive Center** below the Federal breastworks.

*The Cunningham farmhouse, built of logs in the early 1800s, was in the family until purchased by the U.S. Corps of Engineers in the 1970s. It is representative of the "dogtrot"-style house typically found in the South. The two-pen structure is two stories high and has a breezeway in the middle and hand-hewn stone fireplaces with exterior stone chimneys at each end of the house. The house has had many additions over the years including a porch. Siding has been added and the breezeway has been enclosed.

Brooke County

Gen. Isaac Hardin Duval grave, in the Brooke Cemetery; Wellsburg. Duval was born in Wellsburg in 1824. He led an adventurous life in the west until joining the Federal forces as a major of the 1st West Virginia Infantry and later served as a colonel of the 9th West Virginia. He obtained the rank of Brigadier General in September 1864 and participated in Gen. Philip Sheridan's Shenandoah Valley campaign. After the war he was a state senator, U.S. Congressman, state Adjutant General and a collector of Internal Revenue. He died in 1902. *Courtesy Joe Ferrell*

Cabell County

Grave of Brig. Gen. Albert Gallatin Jenkins in the Confederate plot in Spring Hill Cemetery in Huntington. It was moved here from the family plot at Greenbottom in 1891. Jenkins was horn at Greenbottom in 1830, graduated from Jefferson College, Canonsburg, Penn. in 1848, practiced law in Cabell County and was a congressman from western Virginia from 1857 to 1861. He joined the Confederate army at the beginning of the war and fought in western Virginia, Kentucky, Pennsylvania and Virginia where he met his death at the Battle of Cloyd's Mountain on May 9, 1864. Jenkins was the first Confederate officer to plant the Confederate flag in the state of Ohio, made the farthest north advance into Pennsylvania during the Gettysburg campaign, and also served briefly in the First Confederate Congress. *Courtesy Mark Meadows*

The Confederate section in the Spring Hill Cemetery, Huntington.

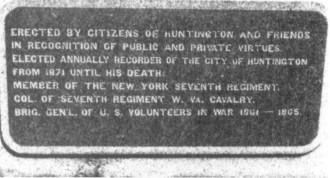

Battle of Barboursville site at the junction of the railroad tracks, Mud River and U.S. Route 60 in Barboursville. A small pitched battle occurred here on July 14, 1861. On that morning, four companies of the 2nd Kentucky Infantry (Federal) marched out of Guyandotte, five miles to the west. They were en route to Scary in Putnam County to disperse an encampment of Confederates. Green militiamen from Cabell and nearby counties were stationed on the long ridge paralleling the Guyandotte River from the town proper to the banks of the Mud River. They awaited the approach of the Federal troops. As the Federal troops emerged from the southern end of the bridge spanning Mud River the Confederates fired on them, killing five and wounding 18. The surprised soldiers hastily took cover under the bridge, behind some abandoned brick kilns and along the banks of the river. From these points they answered the Confederates' fire and finally drove them from the ridge and took the town of Barboursville. The Confederates lost one man and one other was wounded. The wounded man was actually injured in the retreat when he fell into a railroad cut on the ridge. *Courtesy Gary Bays*

McGinnis Home at 101 Main Street in Guyandotte, Cabell County. Built in 1816, it is the second oldest home in the county. It survived the burning of the town and was used as a headquarters by Federal officers occupying the town.

From a painting of Main Street, Barboursville, November 1861.

William C. Miller Home, 1112 Main Street, Barboursville, Cabell County. During a skirmish on Sept. 7, 1862, a charge was made upon this house by Federal troops. A Federal soldier was killed and placed on the house's porch. *Courtesy Joe Geiger, Huntington, WV.*

*Greenbottom** on state Route 2 at Green Bottom in the upper end of the county adjacent to the Ohio River. The house, which was the home of Confederate Brig. Gen. Albert G. Jenkins, was constructed in 1835 by his father, Capt. William Jenkins. Until 1988 the house was privately owned. The U.S. Corps of Engineers bought the property and leased it to the West Virginia Department of Natural Resources, who in turn leased the house to the West Virginia Department of Culture and History which preserves it for its historic integrity. Modern (above) and early 1900s (top) views of Greenbottom. *Courtesy Jack Dickinson*

Brig. Gen. Albert Gallatin Jenkins. *Courtesy Jack Dickinson*

Union Baptist Church, on county Route 25/1, the old James River Turnpike, east of Milton. The church was built in 1849. A Federal garrison occupied the church to protect the one-lane covered bridge which was a vital link on the James River and Kanawha Turnpike. The soldiers left the church in shambles. Bayonet marks, bullet pock marks and a gallery for slaves can still be seen.

*Thomas Carroll House, 234 Guyan Street in Guyandotte. The house was constructed in 1810 in Gallipolis, Ohio, floated down the Ohio River and rebuilt on its present site that same year. In 1835, Thomas Carroll used the house as a church and later as a boarding house and inn for rivermen. Mrs. Carroll's pleas saved the house from burning by Federal troops in 1861.

*Mud River Bridge, located on county Route 25 over the Mud River at Milton. Milton was a small settlement on the James River and Kanawha Turnpike. On April 5, 1863 Confederates under Captain Carpenter tried to take the bridge, but were repulsed. This bridge was probably built in the 1870s to replace the one at the site during the war.

Fayette County

Kanawha Falls, just south of Gauley Bridge on U.S. 60. This is the head of the Kanawha River formed by the junction of the New and Gauley rivers. Prior to the war, mills had been constructed on the north and south ends of the falls. In June 1861 Confederate forces reinforced the mills as defensive positions. Both armies passed by and camped here during the war. *Courtesy Tim McKinney*

The Falls of the Kanawha at present-day Glen Ferris. This painting was reproduced in color in Edward Beyer's *Album of Virginia* in 1857. *Courtesy Virginia State Library*

*Glen Ferris Inn,** on U.S. 60 at Glen Ferris. It was built in 1816 by Aaron Stockton as a major inn on the James River and Kanawha Turnpike. The central unit is the original section of the building, with the wings added after the Civil War. Thousands of troops passed by here during the war and in the fall of 1861 Federal forces used the inn as a quartermaster depot. In November 1861 Confederates fired artillery at the house from the heights of Cotton Hill.

Zoll's Hollow, on U.S. 60 at Glen Ferris. This is the site of a Federal ammo dump that was blown up in September 1862. Shell fragments and bullets can still be found here.

Gauley Bridge Historic Site, at the junction of U.S. 60 and state Routes 16 and 39.

Miller Tavern, located in Gauley Bridge, was used as a Federal army headquarters by General Cox in 1861 and General Lightburn in 1862. It is now a Senior Citizens Center.

This **covered bridge** across the Gauley River was built in 1850 and was destroyed in 1861 by Confederate troops. *Courtesy Fayette County Historical Society*

This photo, taken in 1862, shows the wire suspension bridge which spanned the Gauley River until it was destroyed by Federal troops in September 1862. *Courtesy Aubrey Musick, Gauley Bridge*

Bridge Pier, still standing in the Gauley River, supported at least two bridges destroyed during the war.

The only extant Confederate cannon emplacement on **Cotton Hill**, it is dug into the ridge about 30-by-20-feet with an earthen mound at the front and was dug in 1861 by troops of General Floyd. *Courtesy Tim McKinney*

Fleshman Farm, on state Route 19 at Fayetteville. The utility pole on the right marks the site where 19 Confederate soldiers killed at the Battle of Fayetteville are buried.

View of **Cotton Hill** from Gauley Bridge. This area was the scene of much fighting and many troop movements during the early part of the war, including a six-day artillery duel in November 1861. It was from the ridgetop overlooking Gauley Bridge that the Confederates used a 12-pound bronze cannon to fire on General Lightburn's Federal troops retreating westward in 1862. The Confederates were in such a hurry to get to Gauley Bridge and capture the enemy's left-over supplies that they supposedly threw the cannon into a nearby ravine rather than spend time hauling it off the mountain. Reports of the cannon circulated through the years and in August 1953 the *Charleston Daily Mail* sponsored a major search for it (in which the author participated). The site from which the cannon was fired and a cannon ball were found but there was no trace of the cannon itself. It probably was hauled off for scrap years before if, in fact, it was ever thrown into the ravine in the first place. *Courtesy Tim McKinney*

Isaac Abbot cabin, at Beckwith on Laurel Creek. It was built in 1863 by the family of Capt. Joel H. Abbot, 8th Virginia Cavalry C.S.A. Captain Abbot is buried on the property. *Courtesy Tim McKinney*

Camp Reynolds Site, off county Route 13/2 on the east side of the Kanawha River, just south of Kanawha Falls. This was the winter headquarters (1862-63) of the 23rd Ohio Volunteer Infantry. The 23rd was commanded by Col. Rutherford B. Hayes, and one of the young lieutenants was William McKinley—two future presidents. Rifle pits and trenches can still be traced. The camp was first called Camp Maskell and later the name was changed to honor Maj. Eugene E. Reynolds, who was killed at the Battle of South Mountain.

View of the **Montgomery's Ferry house** below Kanawha Falls, circa 1865. During the Civil War this house was occupied many times by Federal troops. In 1956 the home was destroyed. It is now the site of the Glen Ferris State Road garage. *Courtesy Tim McKinney*

Camp Tompkins Site. Today this is the Hawks Nest Country Club on U.S. 60 between Gauley Bridge and Ansted. The home of prominent area farmer and retired army officer, Col. Christopher Q. Tompkins was located here. The home, "Gauley Mount," one of the finest in the vicinity, was used by Federal Gen. William Rosecrans as army camp and headquarters. Mrs. Tompkins was forced to leave her home and move to Richmond. The house survived the war but was only a shell of its former self, being severely dilapidated.

Van Bibbers Rock, at the Camp Reynolds site. Carving on a rock was made on Nov. 28, 1862, by Jno Day Jr., a member of the 23rd Ohio Volunteer Infantry.

Federal soldiers on Van Bibbers Rock at Camp Reynolds, 1862. *Courtesy Fayette County Historical Society*

Grave of Julia Neale Jackson, located in Westlake Cemetery, Ansted. Confederate memorial services were conducted by members of the 36th Virginia Infantry re-enactment group on June 27, 1987. The sign reads —Here lies the Mother of Stonewall Jackson-Born Feb. 28, 1798, Married first to Jonathan Jackson, Married then to Blake B. Woodson — she died Sept. 1831. This tribute erected by town of Ansted. *Courtesy Tim McKinney*

*Contentment Historic Complex, on U.S. 60, one mile east of Hawks Nest State Park, constructed about 1830 on the James River and Kanawha Turnpike in the west end of present-day Ansted. It was acquired in 1872 by ex-Confederate Col. George W. Imboden. He was commander of the 18th Virginia Cavalry Regiment during the war and later first mayor of Ansted. Imboden is buried in Ansted's Westlake Cemetery. The house, museum and one-room country schoolhouse are operated by the Fayette County Historical Society, 213 Washington Ave., Oak Hill, WV 25901.

Trenches along U.S. 60 near Hawks Nest Country Club, part of Camp Tompkins. Gun emplacements and trenches are located nearby.

*Halfway House, on old U.S. 60, Ansted. It was built around 1810. During the winter of 1862-63 the House was the headquarters of the Chicago Grey Dragoons. VMI Professor Thomas J. Jackson was a guest at the inn while visiting his mother's grave in Ansted on Sept. 1, 1855. It is now privately owned.

Walker Homestead, on county Route 11, about three miles southeast of Lookout, off U.S. 60. This house, which is on the original James River and Kanawha Turnpike, was used as a headquarters by both Federal and Confederate troops in 1861. It is now abandoned.

Early-day photo of the **Halfway House** or **Tyree Tavern** in Ansted. *Courtesy Tim McKinney*

Spy Rock, on U.S. 60 just east of Lookout. Indians named this the "Rock of eyes" because of the great distances visible from this point. During the war troops on both sides posted lookouts here and named it "Spy Rock." *Courtesy Tim McKinney*

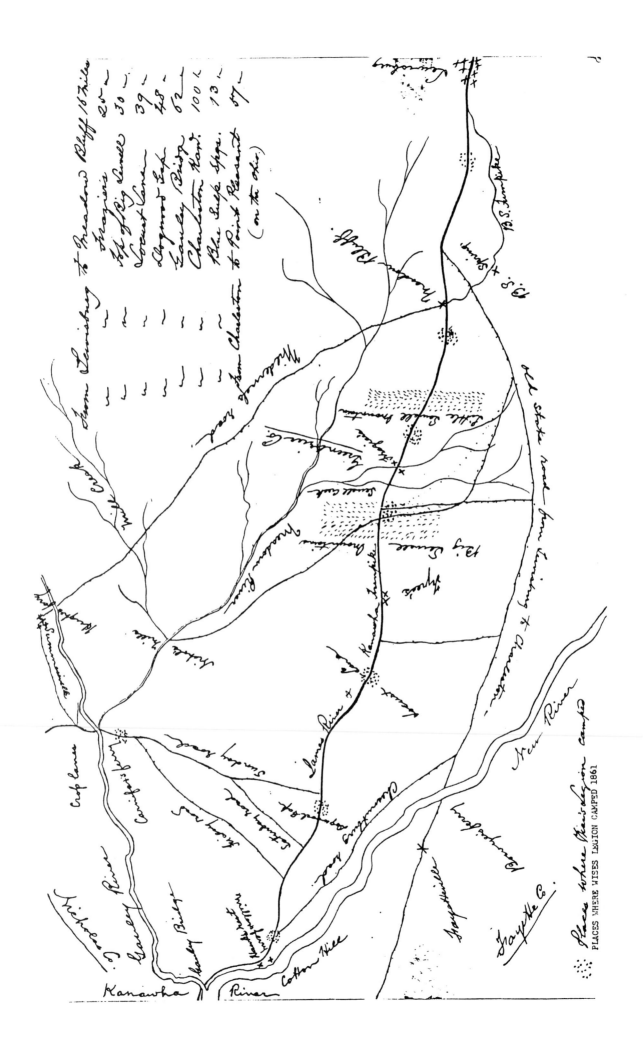

PLACES WHERE WISES LEGION CAMPED 1861

FAYETTE COUNTY
HISTORICAL LANDMARK
1861

THE FAYETTE COUNTY HISTORIC
LANDMARK COMMISSION

CONFEDERATE GEN. ROBERT E. LEE'S
HEADQUARTERS
CAMP COVERED 33 ACRES
OF THIS HILLTOP
SEPT. - OCT. 1861
THE TRENCH VISIBLE HERE IS
ALL THAT REMAINS OF WHAT
ONCE SURROUNDED THIS SITE

Sewell Mountain marker on Myles Knob on Sewell Mountain just off U.S. 60. This marker was dedicated on Sept. 24, 1989 by the Fayette County Historical Society. A military camp was established on the site as a defensive position by Confederate Gen. Henry Wise on Sept. 14, 1861. The objectives of Wise's 7,000 troops were to maintain control of the James River and Kanawha Turnpike and to prevent Federal troops from advancing further east. The Confederates also hoped to draw the enemy into attacking their excellent defensive positions on the mountain. Gen. Robert E. Lee arrived at the camp on September 24, to assume direct command of General Wise's forces and the nearby troops of Gen. John B. Floyd. More than 9,000 men were at Lee's command in the Sewell Mountain area. For three weeks, skirmishes occurred daily between the Confederate and Federal forces as each side attempted to draw the other into battle. In October the Federals withdrew and Lee soon followed. The inclement weather during this period precluded any decisive action by either side. *Courtesy Tim McKinney*

Area occupied as the main **Sewell Mountain headquarters camp** on Myles Knob. The rise in the foreground is a trench dug by Gen. Robert E. Lee's men. *Courtesy David Miles, Charmco, WV.*

Busters Knob, view from the top of Sewell Mountain on U.S. 60. Both armies fortified these hills for several months in the fall of 1861.

General Lee on his horse, "Traveller." Traveller had been born and raised near Blue Sulphur Springs in Greenbrier County. As a colt he was named Jeff Davis and took first prize at the Lewisburg fairs in 1859 and 1860. Lee first saw the spirited young horse when the colt was a four-year-old and he spoke of him admiringly as 'my colt,' but declined to accept him as a gift from Maj. Thomas L. Broun and Capt. Joseph M. Broun. Lee rode the horse for a month, however, and became so attached to the animal that he purchased him for $200 in Confederate currency. Renamed Traveller, the horse served the Southern leader throughout the war. Later, when Lee became president of Washington and Lee University at Lexington, Va., he often rode Traveller about town. On Lee's death in 1870, Traveller, saddled and bridled, walked behind the coffin to the grave. Some years later, while grazing on the campus, he stepped on a rusty nail, tetanus developed, and he died in the brick barn near the President's House on the campus. A feather bed had been placed under him by Washington and Lee students. Traveller's remains were buried May 8, 1871, by the UDC on the grounds of Washington & Lee University.

Lee Tree site, on U.S. 60 atop Sewell Mountain. General Lee pitched his tent under this sugar maple tree in 1861. Photographer Homer Wells took this photo in June 1929. The tree was cut down for the United Daughters of the Confederacy by the Civilian Conservation Corps about 1936 and pieces of it were made into souvenirs. This was the site where Lee first saw the horse, which he eventually bought and named "Traveller." *Courtesy Fayette County Historical Society*

The Lee Tree site today.

*Old Stone Tavern, on Stonehouse Road, two miles off U.S. 60 and one mile off state Route 41 near Babcock State Park. Also known as the Tyree Tavern, it was built in 1824 by Richard Tyree and was a well-known stage stop on the James River and Kanawha Turnpike. During the war the tavern was used as a headquarters by both armies and as a military hospital. The original flooring was replaced in 1920 and during the replacement several cannon balls were found under the house, as well as a few discarded medical instruments.

Beckwith Camps, off state Route 16 at Beckwith. These fields were used as major camps by both sides during the war and were known as Camp Fenwick. On a ridge adjacent to these camps can be found the graves of a Confederate lieutenant and three privates killed in a skirmish near here on Sept. 3, 1861. *Courtesy Tim McKinney*

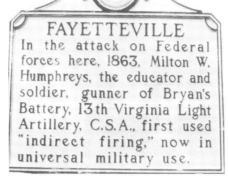

FAYETTEVILLE
In the attack on Federal forces here, 1863, Milton W. Humphreys, the educator and soldier, gunner of Bryan's Battery, 13th Virginia Light Artillery, C.S.A., first used "indirect firing," now in universal military use.

FAYETTEVILLE
In the attack on Federal forces here, 1863, Milton W. Humphreys, the educator and soldier, gunner of Bryan's Battery, 13th Virginia Light Artillery, C.S.A., first used "indirect firing," now in universal military use.

Luther Warner House, at Beckwith. Built in 1856, it was destroyed by fire in 1979. During the war the house was used as a hospital and headquarters for both sides.

Indirect artillery fire *was used for the first time in the history of warfare on May 19 and 20, 1863, from behind a growth of pine trees which stands at Nicholville, 1.3 miles from the Fayette County Courthouse. This location is on the old black top road which is between Fayetteville and Oak Hill. On this spot Corporal Milton W. Humphreys, Bryan's Battery, King's Artillery, C.S.A., successfully fired his rifled cannon with devastating effect upon the Federal fort at Fayetteville a mile away. Humphreys, then but 19, elevated the barrel of the gun so that the trajectory, or path of the cannon shell, would pass above the top of the mask of trees. He knew the approximate range of the piece and the probable distance of the target. The distance of the target from the gun constituted the base of a triangle with the range of the projectile being its hypotenuse. It took the better part of two days for the Yankee commander to figure out where the shells were coming from. Only when an armed patrol was sent out on reconnaissance to locate the source of the shelling was the gun found and those manning it driven off.* From *Historical Notes on Fayette County, W.Va.,* by Rev. C. Shirley Donnelly, 1958.

Remains of earthworks in yard behind the Fayette County Courthouse.

Milton W. Humphries. *Courtesy Washington & Lee University.*

Fayetteville (Fort Scammon site). Remains of earthworks at Dodd and Payne Funeral Home, site of the camp of the 12th Regiment of Ohio Volunteers in April, 1863.

Remains of the Federal Battery McMullen, at Fayetteville near state Route 19 and Laurel Creek Road. These are probably the best-preserved Civil War earthworks in Fayette County. *Courtesy Tim McKinney*

Old Levi Jones House remains, off state Route 16, one mile north of Fayetteville. The house had been used as headquarters and hospital by both armies during the war. Mr. Jones was arrested by Federals as a Confederate Spy. *Courtesy Tim McKinney*

A late 1800s view of the **Levi Jones house**. *Courtesy Tim McKinney*

Cleante Janutolo Spring, on U.S. 21 in Fayetteville. Both armies used this spring as a source of drinking water.

Gilmer County

Fort Moore, on a hill behind the campus of Glenville State College in Glenville. It was built by the Gilmer Home Guards and was burned in 1864 by Confederate troops.

Grant County

Fort Mullegan Site, (above and at right) on State Route 28, just west of Petersburg at Fort Hill. It was constructed by the Federals and is one of the best preserved Civil War forts in the state. Extensive breastworks and trenches are still visible. The site has been restored by the Civil War Preservation Trust with the South Branch Civil War Society, McNeill's Rangers, SCV Camp #582, and 7th West Virginia SCV Camp #7.

Courtesy Civil War Trust

*Hermitage Motor Inn** on state Route 28, U.S. 220 just east of downtown Petersburg. The original Hermitage was built in the early 1840s of bricks fired on the premises with slave labor. It has been in continuous use as a hostelry since 1881. During the war the home was taken over by officers of Federal troops who occupied Petersburg and were stationed at Fort Mullegan.

*The Manor**, off state Route 42 near Petersburg. It was built on lands once owned by Lord Fairfax. This L-shaped structure contains many striking architectural elements both inside and out and was a center of social and political life in the area before and during the Civil War.

Gormania, on U.S. 50 at the Maryland border. This line of trenches, which are in Maryland just across the Potomac River, were part of Fort Pendleton, which was constructed by Federal troops to guard the Northwestern turnpike (present day U.S. 50) which passed through Gormania.

Greenbrier County

*Greenbrier Resort, White Sulphur Springs. One of America's oldest and most elegant resorts was a hospital and rest area for both sides during the war. More than 300 wounded soldiers, both Federal and Confederate, were taken to the hotel after the Battle of White Sulphur Springs. During the June 1864 Federal occupation, the famed resort came perilously close to total destruction. It was saved from the torch only by the quick thinking of a later U.S. Senator, Henry A. DuPont, of Delaware. Sixty years later DuPont recalled that as the troops rested at the resort a rumor passed that Gen. David Hunter had ordered the burning of the entire complex. DuPont was taken aback at the news: "It seemed to me," he wrote, "that the burning of the buildings would be a clear violation not only of the rules of civilized warfare but of the specific instructions of the United States government." Aware that there was no organized resistance in the area, DuPont spent the night devising an argument to convince the tough General Hunter to alter his plans. The next morning they met for breakfast on the lawn and DuPont asked Hunter if the rumors of impending destruction were indeed true. "Yes, I intend to burn them all down," the commander replied, gazing at the hotel and rows of cottages. After a short pause DuPont said, "Don't you think, General, that the burning of these structures would be a military mistake?" He felt a pang of fear when Hunter countered, "What do you mean, Captain, by that inquiry?" DuPont summoned all his courage and answered, "I mean this General —if we have later to occupy and hold this country, the White Sulphur will be the natural point for our principal stations, as so many roads converge here. Such being the case, the buildings as they stand would furnish excellent winter quarters." There was a long silent spell and finally General Hunter changed his mind and countermanded his order. Years after when the DuPonts visited the resort, they were always accorded special treatment in gratitude for this rescue. The resort is now a National Historic Landmark.

View of the 1815 springhouse at The Greenbrier some time after the war. The original statue of Hygeia atop the structure was lost during the war. Many of the cottages and the large President's Cottage still in use at the resort were used by both armies during the war. *The Greenbrier Archives*

Gen. David Hunter (left) and **Captain H.A. DuPont**. *The Greenbrier Archives*

Battle of White Sulphur Springs or **Dry Creek site**, at the intersection of U.S. 60 and state Route 92, one-half mile east of White Sulphur Springs. It was the scene of a two-day engagement between Federal forces under General W.W. Averell and Confederate forces under Maj. Gen. Sam Jones and Col. George S. Patton, Aug. 26-27, 1863. Averell's troops were compelled to retreat on the 27th after their ammunition ran out. Thirteen hundred Federal troops and 2,000 Confederates were engaged with total Federal casualties of 26 killed and 129 wounded and with 20 Confederates killed and 129 wounded. The wounded on both sides were cared for at the Old White Hotel in White Sulphur Springs. The monuments were moved to this site when Route 92 was relocated. The battle monument to the right was erected in 1938 by the Historic Monuments Dedication Committee for the celebration of Greenbrier County's 160th anniversary. Unfortunately the battlefield site behind these markers has now become a large shopping center (1990). The monument to Baron Paul Von Konig, who was killed in this battle, was erected by his New York descendants in 1914.

(Left) **The Greenbrier** about 1859. From *Edward Beyer's Album of Virginia.*

(Below) A post-war photo of the **junction of present U.S. 60 and the Anthony Creek Road**, scene of the Aug. 26-27, 1863 Battle of White Sulphur Springs (also known as Dry Creek, Howard's Creek and Rocky Gap). *West Virginia Dept. of Culture and History*

A shopping center is now located behind the Von Konig Monument.

Von Konig Monument   Nancy Hart Grave

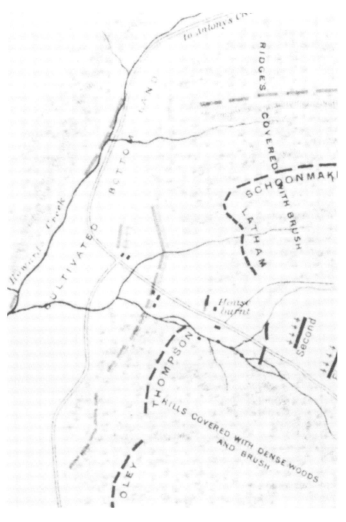

Nancy Hart grave, off county Route 39/1. Nancy Hart, noted Confederate spy, led a surprise attack on Summersville in July 1861. The sweetheart of Perry Connolly, a Confederate guerrilla fighter, Nancy (called Peggy by soldiers of both armies) was a tall, lithe, black-eyed beauty, just 20 years old when she led the attack in which Captain Starr and a Federal force were captured and most of the town burned. When she was later captured, she was charged with espionage and put in the Summersville jail, where her striking beauty and bright roving eyes kept her captors in continual turmoil as they vacillated between duty and desire. Connolly was killed at Welch Glade, and Federal forces gained control of the country around Summersville, making Nancy's escape impossible and her execution apparently certain. Her guards allowed her to roam the jail at will and to walk in the courtyard with a soldier escort on warm evenings. One evening, it is said, the guard succumbed to her charms and allowed her to examine his pistol. She used it to kill him on the spot and then escaped to Confederate territory. After Lee's surrender she returned to marry Joshua Douglas and lived in Greenbrier County until her death in 1902. *Courtesy Ron Hardway, Upper Glade, W.Va.*

Blue Sulphur Springs, on county Route 25 three miles south of Smoot off of I-64 in the southwestern portion of the county. A well-known pre-war health resort, it was used by both armies as a hospital and rest area. In the winter of 1862-63, several hundred Georgia troops were encamped here. Eighty-nine of them died of typhoid fever and were buried on top of a surrounding hill in coffins made out of benches from the cottages and buildings of the resort. In 1864, Federal troops burned the resort and only this Greek-style springhouse remains sitting forlornly in a field.

Organ Cave, on state Route 63, three miles south of Ronceverte near the intersection with U.S. 219. During the war the cave was known as "General Lee's underground powder works" because of the gunpowder made in it. Thirty-seven of the original 52 wooden hoppers used to mine saltpeter, one of the ingredients in gunpowder, are still visible. They were made from local wood and fastened together with wooden pegs. Troughs were hewed from wood to catch the water laden with the nitrate solution, which, in turn, was evaporated to provide the saltpeter. The cave was also used for church services and as a rest area for Confederate troops. It is now a tourist attraction.

The Dietz Farm, at Meadow Bluff just off U.S. 60 near Sam Black Church. This was a major campsite for both armies in this part of the state and General Lee's headquarters in 1861. The house was used as a hospital and has been empty for years. Confederate soldiers are supposedly buried on a nearby hillside. Extensive trenches on nearby Meadow River were dug in 1861 by the 22nd Virginia Infantry Regiment. It is now private property.

* **Valley View Farm**, on U.S. 60, two miles west of Lewisburg. Built in 1828, it was known as Tuckwiller's Tavern during the war. A skirmish was fought on the grounds on May 2, 1863, and the house was used as a hospital and Federal army headquarters. The skirmish was a Federal defeat. The house is now in private hands.

Graves of Confederate soldiers at Blue Sulphur Springs.

UNKNOWN SOLDIERS

Six miles west, a Confederate regt. from Georgia camped at Blue Sulphur Springs in improvised shelters, during the winter of 1863. Many died of exposure and disease, and are buried on the hill 400 yards north of the spring.

*Elmhurst**, at Caldwell on U.S. 60 just east of the Greenbrier River bridge. It was built in 1824 as a stage stop on the James River and Kanawha Turnpike. During the war, a skirmish was fought here following the Battle of Lewisburg. Trenches are still visible on the property.

Brushy Ridge Earthworks, (above and at left) just off I-64 at the Alta exit, west of Lewisburg. Extensive trenches and gun emplacements can still be seen along the ridge for thousands of feet. The 22nd Virginia Infantry constructed these earthworks in early 1862. These are some of the best preserved Civil War fortifications in the state but difficult to get to.

Confederate graves, located on property of The Greenbrier Resort near the Hilltop Tennis Courts. *The Greenbrier Archives*

Bungers Mill site, on county Route 60/11, off old U.S. 60 at the Morlunda Farms, six miles west of Lewisburg. The site of Federal and Confederate encampments throughout the war.

Some of the markers placed around Lewisburg to commemorate the **Battle of Lewisburg**.

Two Civil War cannons are mounted in front of the Old Greenbrier Military Institute, now the West Virginia School of Osteopathic Medicine.

*Former Greenbrier County Library**, 301 Courtney Drive, Lewisburg. It was erected in 1834 by James Frazier as a library and study for the Virginia Court of Appeals. Inside can be seen a section of old plaster where soldiers scratched their names. The county purchased the building in 1939 and restored it to be used as the county library. The adjoining annex was originally a brick slave house from the Johnston Reynolds Mansion. A new county library has been constructed and this building will become a community college library.

Confederate Statue, on the grounds of the former Greenbrier County Library.

*John A. North House, 100 Church Street, Lewisburg, across the street from the library. It was built in 1820 by John Dunn and purchased in 1830 by John Frazier who operated it as the popular Star Tavern for benefit of court attendees. It now houses the museum of the Greenbrier Historical Society.

*David S. Creigh House, also known as "Montescena" located on county Route 37, near Lewisburg. A Greek Revival house built in 1834, "Montescena" was the home of David S. Creigh, a locally prominent individual who became known as "The Martyr of Greenbrier County" to those with southern sympathies. The house was the scene of a tragic episode that resulted in Creigh's "martyrdom" in 1863. Creigh, in the act of defending his home and family, which included a wife and several daughters, from marauding Federal troops, killed one of them. By order of Federal Gen. David Hunter, he was tied behind a horse, made to walk more than 100 miles to Staunton, Virginia and there hanged. It is now a private residence.

*James Withrow House, 220 North Jefferson Street, Lewisburg. It was built in 1818. James Withrow was a Confederate officer and when Federal troops came looking for him, he hid for several days in a secret room in the attic. At the same time, the stair treads were supposedly pried loose and wheat was hidden beneath them. The silverware was buried under the front portico steps.

Jessie Bowlin House, 300 E. Washington Street, Lewisburg. This original log cabin was built in 1784 and used for many purposes through the years including a commissary during the war.

*John Wesley Methodist Church**, 209 East Foster Street, Lewisburg. This handmade brick building was built in 1820 with additions made in 1835. During the May 23, 1862, Battle of Lewisburg a cannonball struck the southwest corner of the church.

*Gov. Samuel Price House**, 224 No. Court Street, Lewisburg. The house was built in 1840. Price represented Greenbrier County in the Virginia constitutional conventions of 1850 and 1860. In 1863 he was elected lieutenant governor of Virginia. He served as the president of the 1872 West Virginia constitutional convention and was appointed to the U.S. Senate in 1876. It is now privately owned.

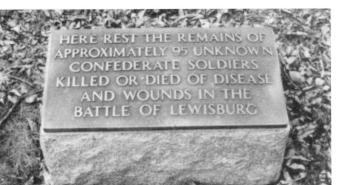

*Confederate Cemetery**, about one-quarter mile up McElhenny Street from the Lewisburg Visitors Center. The remains of 95 unknown Confederate soldiers killed in the Battle of Lewisburg are buried here in a cross-shaped common grave. Initially interred at the Old Stone Church, they were reburied here a few years after the battle.

*Old Stone Presbyterian Church and Cemetery**, 200 Church Street, Lewisburg. Originally built in 1796, it is the oldest church west of the Alleghenies that has remained in continuous use. It served as a hospital during the war. Several Civil War soldiers' graves are located in the adjacent cemetery.

Gen. Alexander Welch Reynolds grave, in the Old Stone Church graveyard in Lewisburg. There is much controversy about the Confederate general even as to his birthplace—Lewisburg or Clarke County, Virginia—either 1815, 1816 or 1817. He graduated from West Point in 1838 and spent his military career in Florida, Mexico and the Midwest. He served in West Virginia under Gen. John Royd and participated in the Fort Donelson, Vicksburg and Atlanta campaigns attaining the rank of brigadier general. After the war his family, including his son, who was a Confederate officer, went to Egypt to join the forces of Ismail Pasha, the Khedive. His son died in 1874 and Reynolds died in Egypt in 1876. An inscription on the Patton vault in the Lewisburg Cemetery states that Reynolds is buried there, but no evidence supports this to date. *Courtesy Joe Ferrell*

Tombstones in the Old Stone Presbyterian Church.

Hampshire County

This unusual grave marker was placed in the cemetery, in 1904, by survivors of the Battle of Dry Creek. It reads: Lt. John Gay Carr, Co. H, 22nd Rgt., Va. Vol. Infty., Kanawha Riflemen. . . Killed in Battle of Dry Creek, Aug. 26, 1861, Aged 31 Years.

General Lewis Motor Inn, 301 East Washington Street in Lewisburg. Part of this popular inn was built prior to the war.

*Capon Springs**, on county Route 16 off of state Route 259 in the southeastern corner of the county. This popular resort (spa) was in operation prior to 1800. The hotel, named "Mountain House," built around 1850, was one of the largest structures in the South. It burned down in 1911. Robert E. Lee and his wife were visiting the spa in 1859 when he was called to Harpers Ferry to put down the attack by John Brown. In 1861, with the war coming and the resort $8,000 in debt, the state ordered the place sold, however, the new state of West Virginia took it over, and Capon Springs became part of the debt that West Virginia owed Virginia after the war. It is still a popular, but private, resort.

Bloomery Gap Skirmish, on U.S. 45, three miles west of Bloomery. Federal forces attacked Confederates on Feb. 14, 1862, and routed them. The Confederates fled toward Winchester, Virginia, but soon returned to the gap when the Federals returned to their camp at Paw Paw.

*Sloan-Parker House** (The Stone House), on U.S. 50 just past the Moorefield junction. This large, finely built stone structure was erected in 1790 by Richard Sloan, patriarch of one of Hampshire County's most prominent families. The home has been used over the years as a stage stop and polling place. It passed to the Parker family in 1854 and was used by both armies during the war. It is now a private residence.

Fort Mill Ridge—this well-preserved earthen fortification was built between March and June 1863. Builders of the fort included the 54th Pennsylvania Infantry and the 1st West Virginia Infantry. The site had previously been used by Confederate artillery to defend approaches to Romney. When Col. Jacob M. Campbell (54th PVI) garrisoned Union forces at Romney, camps were set up at Mechanicsburg Gap. This site was more easily defended by the fort commanding the Northwestern Turnpike which became Route 50.

Location: Two miles west of Romney.

*Sycamore Dale**, on county Route 8 just off U.S. 50, state Route 28, at the crossing of the South Branch of the Potomac River just southwest of Romney. The house was built between 1836 and 1839. Federal Col. Lew Wallace, author of *Ben Hur*, reportedly used the house as his headquarters. McNeill's Rangers surrendered to Federal troops here in 1865. It is now a private residence.

Sign at Capon Bridge.

Blue's Gap Battle, on U.S. 50, eight miles west of Capon Bridge.

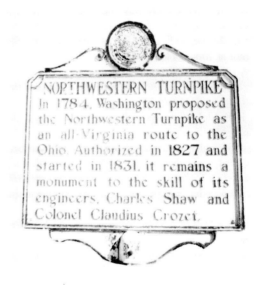

Romney Classical Institute, at the east end of Romney on U.S. 50. It was built in 1846 by the Literary Society of Romney and was used by both sides during the war. It is now part of the West Virginia School for the Deaf and Blind.

Confederate Monument, in the Indian Mound Cemetery on the west end of Romney just off U.S. 50. In 1866 the Confederate Memorial Association was formed in Romney to erect a monument to the soldiers of Hampshire County. Money was raised by sewing bees and fairs, and the monument was ordered in 1867 from Baltimore. With feelings about the war still very intense and the fear that Federal sympathizers would destroy the monument, the inscription was left off until the last moment before it was boxed up and shipped hurriedly to Romney. It was dedicated on Sept. 26, 1867 and is thought to be the first monument erected to Confederate dead in the country. Governor J.J. Jacob, the first Democratic governor of West Virginia after the war is also buried here.

The Occupations of Romney

Romney exchanged hands at least 56 times during the war. Perhaps many more times which are simply not recorded. Most of these involved either one side or the other simply marching into town but sometimes a skirmish would precede the occupation. The following is a brief description of the 56 changes on record*

March 3, 1862, Colonel Downey of the Union army, occupied Romney after General Loring, who had been left here by Jackson, marched back to Winchester. For the next four captures the dates cannot be definitely fixed.

Spring 1862, Hampshire militia occupied when Colonel Downey withdrew.

Summer 1862, Colonel Greenfield, with the 22nd Pennsylvania Regiment, Hampshire militia, or troops from the regular Confederate army, occupied Romney after the Pennsylvanians had retired.

Fall 1862, General Lander sent Maryland troops (Federal) to Romney.

November 1862, General Imboden occupied the town with a Confederate force.

Dec. 29, 1862, General Milroy, with a strong Federal force, occupied the town for a day or two, as he was marching to Winchester.

During the first four months of 1863 there is no record that troops of either side entered the town. That was a time of military activity, however, and in all probability Romney changed hands several times during these months.

June 7 (probably), 1863, Captain McNeill, with a Confederate force, was in possession.

June 15, 1863, Colonel Campbell came in with a Federal force.

June 16, 1863, General Imboden occupied Romney on his march to Gettysburg.

June 17, 1863, a Federal company was in possession of the town for one hour.

June 18, 1863, a Confederate force took possession then hurried on to join the forces on the march to Gettysburg. It is believed that these men belonged to Imboden's brigade and that they had been scouting in the mountains of Hardy County.

June 1863, a Federal cavalry company entered Romney.

June 22, (probably), 1863, Lieutenant Summers, with a Federal force, took possession after Captain Sheetz withdrew.

July 12, 1863, a Confederate force again took possession.

Aug. 8, 1863, Romney occupied by Federal cavalry.

Aug. 15 (probably), 1863, Confederates entered Romney.

September 1863, Federal troops, known as Blinker's Dutch, captured the place.

Oct. 5, 1863, a Confederate force was again in possession.

October 1863, Federal cavalry held the town for a short time. There is no record of further occupation of the town in 1863.

Jan. 5, 1864, McNeill was in possession of Romney.

Jan. 8, 1864, Federal cavalry entered and took possession.

Feb. 1, 1864, Confederate cavalry held the town.

Feb. 1, 1864, New York cavalry drove out the Confederates.

Feb. 3, 1864, the town was in possession of Confederates belonging to General Rosser's command.

Feb. 3, 1864, General Averell, who was hunting for Rosser, took the town.

May 10, 1864, McNeill was once more in possession.

May 10, 1864, McNeill departed and Federal troops were in possession.

May 10, 1864, the Confederates, whether McNeill or not cannot be ascertained, drove out the Federals, making three times in one day that Romney changed hands.

July 1864, Federal cavalry under Ringgold held the town.

Aug. 5, 1864, General McCausland occupied Romney on his return from his raid into Pennsylvania.

Aug. 5, General Averell passed through Romney in pursuit of McCausland, having been only two hours behind him when McCausland set fire to Chambersburg, and having been in pursuit all the way to Romney. He overtook and defeated him at Moorefield.

Aug. 29, 1864, McNeill occupied Romney.

Oct. 31, 1864, Federal cavalry from Springfield occupied the place.

Nov. 1, 1864, McNeill occupied the town on his way to attack Springfield.

Nov. 2, 1864, Federals pursuing McNeill entered Romney.

Nov. 28, 1864, Confederates belonging to General Rosser's force occupied the town, the day that Keyser was captured.

January 1865, Federal troops from Cumberland were in the town.

Feb. 1, 1865, a force of 200 Confederates were in possession of Romney.

Feb. 5, 1865, Colonel Young with a Federal force were in the town.

Feb. 7 (probably), 1865, McNeill held the town.

Feb. 13, 1865, the Federals were once more in possession.

Feb. 19, 1865, McNeill was once more in possession, carrying away Generals Crook and Kelley as prisoners, having captured them at Cumberland, Maryland.

Feb. 19, 1865, Federal cavalry, pursuing McNeill, were in town about one hour.

Feb. 25 (probably), 1865, Federals from Cumberland were in possession.

April 15 (probably), 1865, the town was held for the last time by armed Confederates. They were the companies of McDonald and Sheetz, who had escaped from Virginia when General Lee surrendered.

*Taken from *Historic Hampshire, A Symposium of Hampshire County and Its People, Past and Present*. Edited by Selden W. Brannon, McClain Publishing Co., Parsons, W.Va.., 1976

Old Wirgman Building site, on Main Street in Romney. The Bank of the South Branch of the Potomac was established here about 1800. A bank building was built here in 1825 and it was from that building that Confederate Lieutenant John Blue, a spy for Stonewall Jackson, made a daring escape on April 20, 1862, when Romney was occupied by Federal troops. The site is now the Bank of Romney.

Stonewall Jackson's Headquarters, on state Route 28 just across the street from the entrance to the School for the Deaf and Blind in Romney. This house was the headquarters for Gen. Thomas J. "Stonewall" Jackson during his stay in Romney in 1862. Jackson threatened to resign from the Confederate army when the Secretary of War frustrated his plans for holding the town of Romney in 1862. He wrote the following to the Secretary:

"Your order requiring me to direct General Loring to return with his command to Winchester immediately has been received and promptly complied with. With such interference with my command I cannot expect to be of much service in the field, and accordingly respectfully request to be ordered to report for duty to the superintendent of the Virginia Military Institute at Lexington, as has been done in the case of other professors. Should this application not be granted, I respectfully request that the president will accept my

resignation from the army. I am sir, very respectfully, your obedient servant. TJ. Jackson."

To Governor Letcher, Jackson wrote:

"Governor: This morning I received an order from the secretary of war to order General Loring and his command to fall back from Romney to Winchester immediately. The order was promptly complied with, but, as the order was given without consulting me, and is abandoning to the enemy what has cost much preparation, expense and exposure to secure, and is in direct conflict with my military plans, and implies a want of confidence in my capacity to judge when General Loring's troops should fall back, and is an attempt to control military operations in detail from the secretary's desk at a distance, I have, for the reason set forth in the accompanying paper, requested to be ordered to the institute; and if this is denied me, then to have my resignation accepted. I ask as a special favor that you will have me ordered back to the institute. As a single order like that of the secretary's may destroy the entire fruits of a campaign, I cannot reasonably expect, if my operations are thus to be interfered with, to be of much service in the field. A sense of duty brought me into the field and thus far kept me. It now appears to be my duty to return to the institute, and I hope you will leave no stone unturned to get me there. If I have ever acquired, through the blessings of Providence, any influence over troops, this undoing of my work by the secretary may greatly diminish my influence. I regard the recent expedition as a great success. Before our troops left here, January 1, there was not, so far as I have been able to ascertain, a single loyal man in Morgan County who could remain at home in safety. In four days that county was entirely evacuated by the enemy; Romney and the most valuable portion of Hampshire County were recovered without the firing of a gun, and before we had ever entered the county. I desire to say nothing against the secretary of war. I take it for granted that he has done what he believed to be best, but I regard such a policy ruinous. TJ. Jackson"

Jackson consented to have his resignation withdrawn from the files of the war office upon an apologetic letter from the governor. In an effort to keep the story of his resignation from Confederate troops, all correspondence regarding it was placed in the hands of Governor Letcher. Although these papers were lost when the Confederates retreated from Richmond in April 1865, they were later found where they had been hidden by Governor Letcher's mother.

Hardy County

*John T. Mathias Homestead, 13 miles south of Baker on Route 259 near the entrance to Lost River State Park. Built in 1797 and added on to in 1825, this house was built and owned for generations by the Mathias family for whom the village was named. In 1974 it was purchased by the Mathias Civic Center Association. During the war the house was used by Federal troops who burned holes in an upstairs floor.

The Four Winds, four miles north of Wardensville, on the left, Route 259. A log home originally built in 1825 at Wardensville. It was used as a school in 1825 and a hospital during the war. Later it became a blacksmith shop and a home. It was moved to its present site and rebuilt in 1948. Now it's a private residence.

Skirmish at the bridge across the South Branch of the Potomac River at Romney, June 13, 1861. From a contemporary sketch by Gookins of the 11th Indiana Infantry in *Harpers Weekly*, July 6, 1861. *WV Department of Culture & History*

*The Willows, two miles south of Moorefield on U.S. 220, then left on Cold Springs Road. Formerly the "Randolph Place" where Confederate Maj. Harry Gilmor was captured in 1865. It is now a private residence.

*Mill Island, near Moorefield, on county Route 7, east on Winchester Avenue to the railroad, then south on South Fork Road 1.5 miles to a lane on the right. Built about 1847 by Felix Seymour, this is where county records were hidden from Federal troops during the war. It's now a private residence.

Maslin House, on U.S. 220 at the south end of Moorefield. This house was built in 1848 by Thomas Maslin, a prominent man in the area. When Moorefield was occupied by Federal forces, several Confederate sympathizers were hidden in a secret chamber of the house. It is now a private residence.

*Presbyterian Church, on Main Street in Moorefield. Built in 1847, it was used by both sides as a hospital during the war. Federal troops stabled their horses here, for which the United States government paid indemnity 50 years later.

S.A. McMechen House, on Main Street in Moorefield. A private residence during the war where Gen. John McCausland was staying when he was alerted to Gen. William Averell's surprise attack at Old Fields on Aug. 7, 1864. It is now a bed and breakfast inn with a McCausland room.

***Willow Wall**, on U.S. 220 at Old Fields. This three-story brick home was built in 1818 by Capt. Daniel McNeill. During the war the house was the base of operations of the McNeill Rangers, led by Capt. Hanson McNeill and his son, Jesse. The elder McNeill enlisted a company of less than 200 men for independent service for the Confederacy in the South Branch Valley. By their daring exploits the Rangers inflicted more damage on the Federal forces than the entire Confederate regiments in the area. The Rangers destroyed miles of railroad track, blew up bridges, captured train loads of supplies and burned railroad cars. They also captured hundreds of prisoners, animals and munitions. They operated throughout the Eastern Panhandle and occasionally into Maryland. Daniel McNeill was killed in a raid near Mount Jackson, Virginia, in October 1864 by a member of his own unit. His son, Jesse, took command. On one daring raid in February 1865, the Rangers rode 90 miles through enemy-occupied territory and arrived in Cumberland, Maryland, shortly after midnight. There they surprised the troops stationed in town, made prisoners of the picket guards, and proceeded to the Federal headquarters where they captured Gens. Benjamin Kelley and George Crook. They then made a 60-mile dash for Confederate lines and successfully eluded a force of 2,000 cavalrymen who chased after them. On Aug. 7, 1864, the Battle of Moorefield was fought in the vicinity of the house. Now a private residence.

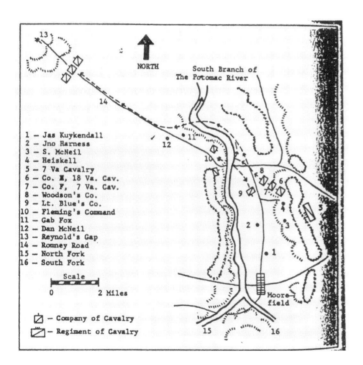

Skirmish at Moorefield, November 27, 1864.

Harrison County

Stonewall Jackson's Statue, on the front lawn of the Harrison County Courthouse in Clarksburg at the corner of West Main and South Third streets. The statue points directly at Jackson's birthplace site across the street. It was placed here in 1953.

Lowndes Municipal Park, on Lowndes Hill in Clarksburg, the entrance is at the south end of South Second Street. Federal forces fortified this area during the war and trenches are still visible today.

Baltimore & Ohio R. R. Telegraph.

BY TELEGRAPH,

Dated Clarksburg June 30. 1861
Received   o'clock   min.   M.

To Genl Morris

                    Rebels companies
we threw captured killing men Schleick
four seventh occupied supply ordnance
wagons delayed of move morning night
companies Buckhannon in rebels and
to wedge bridge they are but many
one fought ten " regiments. Glenville
Weston waver train stores by wagon
with seventh part surprised last near
near cavalry wounding young disposed
communicate tomorrow all left Elk scouts
horse Lieutenant 6 miles in wild two last
early well want and large Ohio of reply
night Irving warm yesterday several
party with three well.

                    G. B. McClellan
                            Maj! Genl

Stonewall Jackson's Birthplace, 328 West Main Street, Clarksburg. Jackson was born in a small brick house at this site on Jan. 21, 1824.

HEADQUARTERS, CHEAT MOUNTAIN DIVISION, }
Clarksburg, Virginia, Oct. 22, 1861.   }

GENERAL ORDERS—

No. 28. The General Commanding has been repeatedly pained to learn that a few bad men in some of the Regiments of his command, are in the habit of abusing, beating, and otherwise maltreating the negro and mulatto servants and teamsters employed by officers and quartermasters in his command. The services of these negroes and mulattos are necessary and cannot be dispensed with, without taking soldiers from their legitimate duties, which would be an injury to the service. These black people are generally quiet and orderly—they were created black and cannot help it—they have mostly been made slaves, and robbed of the proceeds of their own labor, and could not help it; and have left traitor masters in arms against our forces, and are desirous of helping us all they can; and are, therefore, entitled to our pity and commiseration, rather than abuse and contempt; and none but traitors or a coward who would strike a woman and abuse children would wantonly maltreat them. It is suspected that the rebels have hired these bad men to enlist in some of our regiments as spies, and for the purpose of abusing and driving back the contrabands, that they (the rebels) may have the benefit of the services of their slaves, and they be deterred from coming into our lines.

    It is therefore ordered, and hereby made the duty of every officer and soldier of this command, to immediately shoot down every soldier or other person, who may be found causelessly abusing, beating, or otherwise maltreating any of the negro or mulatto servants, or drivers in or about this command.

                    By order of

                    BRIGADIER GENERAL R. H. MILROY.

                    HENRY C. FLESHER,

                    Capt. & A. A. A. Gen.

Jackson Cemetery, East Pike Street between Cherry Street and Charleston Avenue in Clarksburg. The plot was granted by the Jackson family as a public cemetery in 1808. Enclosed by an iron picket fence are the graves of Stonewall

Jackson's great-grandparents, his father and sister, and Mrs. Mary Payne Jackson and Mrs. Mary Coles Payne, sister and mother of Dorothy (Dolley) Madison.

Jackson County

This broadside was distributed by Gen. Henry A. Wise on his July 1861 raid to Ripley. It was probably printed in advance in Charleston as there was no printing facility in Ripley at the time. The *Virginia Chronicle* plant was located at Ravenswood, 15 miles north but the Confederates did not reach there as four companies of Ohio troops occupied the town. *SWV*

Buffington Island, in the Ohio River just north of Ravenswood. This was the scene on July 19, 1863 of the only battle fought in the state of Ohio, between Federal troops and Confederate troops under Gen. John Morgan. The ford extending between the island and the Virginia shore was known to be one of the best on the Ohio, and it was toward it that the daring Confederate general, led his men as he raced across southern Ohio during the summer of 1863. Closely pursued by the Federals, it was Buffington Island's ford which Morgan hoped would provide his escape route from Yankee territory back to the South. He arrived on the Ohio shore across from the island late on July 18, but the next day before he could effect a crossing for his 2,000 exhausted men, the northern forces were upon him. All that Sunday morning the battle raged; its conclusion saw Morgan utterly defeated and the greater part of his men either killed or taken prisoners of war. While he managed to escape northward and elude capture for a few more days, the raid he had so gallantly led had come to an ignoble end. About 30 raiders actually succeeded in crossing the river. To cut off the escape of any more, and to harass the Confederates on the mainland battlefield, three Northern gunboats which had rushed upriver to join the fray, the *Imperial*, the *Moose* and the *Allegheny Belle*, steamed up the Ohio channel of the island raking the Ohio shore with murderous fire. This action has been credited by historians as being the only naval battle to take place in West Virginia and it occurred in waters of Buffington Island.

Jefferson County

*Harpers Ferry Complex

Harpers Ferry developed from a tiny village in the mid-1700s into an industrialized community. The town received its first real impetus in the 1790s when President George Washington urged Congress to establish a national armory here along the Potomac. The armory supported the economy of the town and encouraged the establishment of small industries on adjacent Virginius Island. The arrival of the Chesapeake and Ohio Canal and the Baltimore and Ohio Railroad in the 1830s assured Harpers Ferry of the economic success it was to enjoy well past mid-century. Then came disaster. In October 1859 John Brown's raid jarred the peaceful town, and the Civil War that followed 18 months later was to leave a path of destruction that wrecked the towns economy. The armory and arsenal buildings were burned in 1861 to keep them from falling into Confederate hands. Because of the towns geographical location and its railway system, Federal and Confederate troop movements through Harpers Ferry were frequent, and soldiers of both armies occupied the town intermittently throughout the war. The largest military operation against Harpers Ferry occurred prior to the Battle of Antietam in September 1862 when Confederate forces under Gen. Thomas J. "Stonewall" Jackson seized the town and captured the 12,500-man Federal garrison commanded by Col. Dixon Miles.

Shenandoah Street, looking west. The buildings in the foreground have been restored and several are now museums. The National Park Service Visitors Center is at the end of the row of buildings in the background.

High Street, looking north. Several of these buildings have been restored to their wartime look.

Bridge Piers, in the Potomac River. These are the remains of a railroad bridge built before the Civil War and destroyed in 1861.

John Brown's Fort, just off Shenandoah Street. This is the enginehouse where John Brown made his famous stand against the Marines in 1859. When the armory was burned during the war this was the only building left standing, and after the war it was an attraction for sightseers. In 1892 it was dismantled and shipped to the World's Columbian Exposition at Chicago. After the exposition it was sold and would have been used for a stable if a group led by Miss Kate Field, an actress, had not raised funds to buy it and have it shipped back to Harpers Ferry. It was rebuilt two miles from town and stood on an obscure site until 1910 when it was moved to the campus of Storer College west of town. Although "bricks from John Brown's Fort" have been sold to tourists ever since the War between the States, the structure is believed to contain the greater part of its original brickwork. It was moved to its present site in the 1960s, just a short distance from its original site.

John Brown Monument, above Potomac Street. The white obelisk was erected in 1895 by the Baltimore & Ohio Railroad on the site of the enginehouse in which John Brown and his raiders made their stand. To the left of the monument is a row of five bronze tablets describing the capture of Harpers Ferry by Stonewall Jackson on Sept. 15, 1862.

John Brown's Fort at its original site sometime after the Civil War.

A portion of **Harpers Ferry** in 1899. The monument, erected in 1895 on a 15-foot high railroad embankment, is at the site of the armory's enginehouse. The base of the monument is about where the enginehouse's cupola would have been. St. Peter's Church, in the background, had just been remodeled.

KOA Trenches, located at the KOA campground to the north of Harpers Ferry off U.S. 340.

Master Armorer's House, on Shenandoah Street. Built in 1858 as the home for the chief gunsmith of the armory, it is now a museum where the story of gunmaking is told.

St. Peter's Roman Catholic Church, on the hill above the stone steps. The church was built in 1830 and extensively remodeled in 1896. During the war it was the only church in town that conducted regular services undisturbed by both armies because Father Michael Costello emphasized its neutrality by flying both Confederate and Union flags.

* **Stonewall Jackson's Headquarters**, on Washington Street in Bolivar. It was built in 1795 by Gen. "Lighthorse Harry" Lee. The house became Jackson's headquarters in 1861 for a short time.

John Brown's Raid

In the summer of 1859 a party of men, led by an austere old man who called himself Isaac Smith, appeared in the vicinity of Harpers Ferry, established headquarters at the Kennedy Farm on the Maryland side of the Potomac River, and under the pretense of prospecting for minerals in the nearby hills perfected plans for an attack on the slavery system. On the night of Oct. 16, 1859, Isaac Smith revealed himself to be John Brown, already widely known as "Osa-watomie Brown" of the bloody anti-slavery warfare in Kansas. According to his biographer, W.E.B. DuBois, John Brown chose Harpers Ferry for many reasons, his love of beauty among them. DuBois writes: "He chose Harper's Ferry because a United States arsenal was there and the capture of this would give that dramatic climax to the inception of his plan which was so necessary to its success. But both these were minor reasons. The foremost and decisive reason was that Harpers Ferry was the safest natural entrance to the Great Black Way —One has but to glance at the mountains and swamps of the South to see the Great Black Way. Here, amid the mighty protection of overwhelming numbers, lay a path from slavery to freedom, and along that path were fastnesses and hiding-places easily capable of becoming permanent fortified refuges for organized bands of determined armed men."

Brown, who claimed he was an "instrument of God sent to liberate all slaves" was a terror to pro-slavery settlers in the west, and during his active career as an abolitionist many believed he was insane.

John Brown

After a short speech to his 22 followers, six or seven of whom were Negroes, John Brown marched upon Harpers Ferry while the town slept, captured and imprisoned two watchmen, and took possession of the Government armory. The raiders also seized as hostages several prominent citizens, among them Col. Lewis Washington of Beall-Air. The first man killed was a free Negro, Heywood Shepherd, a railroad porter who was shot by Brown's men when he failed to obey an order to halt. With the raiders in possession of the large stock of arms, the town was at their mercy, and Brown confidently awaited the arrival of the arms and ammunition train, which according to his plan were to follow him. Brown's men boarded the Baltimore & Ohio westbound train and delayed it until early morning. When it was allowed to proceed, it spread the alarm.

Wild rumors spread through the countryside the next morning, and by noon companies of militia from Charles

Town, Martinsburg, Shepherdstown, Winchester and other communities converged upon the town. Citizens with squirrel rifles and other assorted firearms were already exchanging shots with the raiders. By evening all avenues of escape were cut off, and Brown, with his men and prisoners, took refuge in the enginehouse of the armory, still hopeful that reinforcements would arrive. Late that night Brevet Col. Robert E. Lee and Lieutenant J.E.B. Stuart arrived from Washington with 90 Marines. At daybreak, when Brown refused to surrender, the Marines stormed the fort, using a battering ram to break down the door. In the raid, 10 of Brown's command were killed, including two of his sons, four townsmen, and one Marine. Twelve were wounded. Five of the insurrectionists escaped, but Brown and six others were captured and thrown in the county jail at Charles Town. Brown was indicted for treason against Virginia, tried, and hanged at Charles Town. The seizure of Harpers Ferry and the attempt to encourage slave rebellion were recognized by fervent abolitionists as the beginning of the conflict soon to come. Even southern leaders feared its effects and expressed the belief that the sympathy Brown gained in his role as martyr to the cause would serve to forward it.

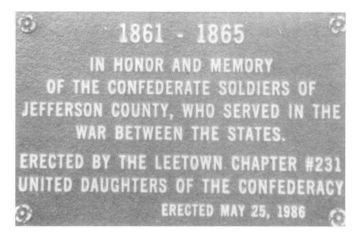

Old Jail site, southwest corner of South George and West Washington streets in Charles Town. On this site, now occupied by the post office, stood the Jefferson County Jail from about 1803 to 1922. Here John Brown was incarcerated in 1859.

*****Jefferson County Courthouse**, (left) corner of North George and East Washington streets in Charles Town. Built in 1836 to replace the original building from 1808. During the war the court records were removed by wagon to Lexington, Virginia, and the courthouse was damaged by shellfire. The building was used as a barracks for Federal troops. It was extensively remodeled in 1871-72 and the records reinstalled. A wing to the rear was added in 1916. The building was the scene of one of the most famous treason trials in the United States-John Browns Trial of 1859.

*John Brown's hanging site, on South Samuel Street, between McCurdy Street and Beckwith Alley in Charles Town. Here John Brown was executed on Dec. 2, 1859. *Courtesy Dave Gilbert*

Bolivar Methodist Church, on Washington Street in Bolivar. This church was used as a hospital during the war.

Bolivar, adjacent to Harpers Ferry on the west. Originally known as Mudfort, the town's name was changed to Bolivar in 1825, in honor of the South American liberator, Simon Bolivar. During the war, both Federal and Confederate forces repeatedly occupied the town. The heights above Bolivar provided a natural vantage point for defending the area from troops advancing from the west towards Harpers Ferry.

Superintendant's House in Harpers Ferry, Jefferson County.

Rutherford House, corner of East Washington and Seminary streets, Charles Town, Jefferson County. Thomas and Mary Rutherford were the owners during the Civil War. They were hosts to a meeting between Gen. Ulysses S. Grant and Gen. Phillip Sheridan on Sept. 17, 1864, in the "East Parlor," now the dining room. The home is now a bed and breakfast called the Carriage Inn.

*Beall-Air (Col. Lewis William Washington Home), off county Route 24 near Halltown. The main structure dates from 1820, and was constructed by Col. Lewis William Washington, great-grand-nephew of George Washington. Colonel Washington was taken prisoner by John Brown in his raid on Harpers Ferry in 1859. The home passed out of the Washington family in 1877. Now it's a private residence.

*The Bower, on county Route 1/1 near Leetown. Built in 1805 and home to the locally prominent Dandridge family, this place was the site, in the fall of 1862, of one of the most romantic and most famous "interludes" of the war. Here, after the Battle of Antietam, renowned Confederate cavalry leader General J.E.B. Stuart and his staff camped on the grounds and in the front yard for nearly three weeks. The general and staff spent the time dancing and picnicking with the Dandridge girls and other local beauties, enjoying a needed rest and "idyll" before resuming wartime activities. It is now a private residence.

*Locust Hill, on U.S. 51, three miles west of Charles Town. This mansion was built in 1840 by John B. and Lucy Washington Packette. The house still shows signs of battle during Confederate Gen. Jubal A. Early's 1864 Shenandoah Valley campaign.

*Richwood Hall (Lawrence Augustine Washington House), off county Route 51/1 near Charles Town. It was built in 1820 on Washington family land. Confederate Gen. Jubal A. Early's men camped here during the Battle of Cameron's Depot in 1864. Now it's a private residence.

*Elmwood (Edward Lucas III House), off county Route 17 near Shepherdstown. Built by Revolutionary War soldier Edward Lucas III in 1797, it was used as a hospital during the war. It is now a private residence.

*Blakeley, off county Route 13/3 near Charles Town. It was built in 1820 by John Augustine Washington II, who inherited Mount Vernon in 1829. His son, John Augustine Washington III sold Mount Vernon in 1859 and was killed at Elkwater, Randolph County in 1861 while serving on Gen. Robert E. Lee's staff. The house suffered from fire in 1864 but was rebuilt. It was later the home of Col. R. Preston Chew, commander of the horse artillery of the Army of Northern Virginia. It is now a private residence.

*Rion Hall, off U.S. Route 340, Halltown, near Charles Town. Built in 1836 by Congressman William Lucas, this was the home of Judge Daniel B. Lucas, a captain in Wise's Legion of Confederate forces, best friend of famed Confederate officer John Yates Beall, and author of the paeon to life in the South, *The Land Where We Were Dreaming*. In 1864 it was the headquarters of Federal Gen. Philip H. Sheridan and his staff. Saber marks said to have been put there by Sheridan's staff officers may still be seen on the parlor's mantle. It is now a private residence.

*Strider Farm, on state Route 27, west of Harpers Ferry. This farm was the site of several important actions during the Civil War. In 1862, during the pre-Antietam campaign, Poague's Artillery (C.S.A.) was positioned here as was the brigade of Col. John W. Brockenbrough during the engagement that brought about the surrender to the Federal army in Harpers Ferry. In 1864, the home served as the headquarters of Federal Gen. Horatio G. Wright during the opening of the Shenandoah campaign. It is now a private residence.

The old cement mill on River Road, about one mile downstream from Shepherdstown and about one quarter mile upstream from Pack Horse Ford. It is the site of the Battle of Cement Mill. The Cement Mill property is now owned by the Jefferson County Historic Landmarks Commission. It is composed of 18 acres. The Shepherdstown Battlefield Preservation Association, Inc. was organized in 2004 to preserve the 1862 Battle of Shepherdstown. For info: www. battleofshepherdstown.org. *Courtesy Dave Gilbert*

*Pack Horse Ford, on German Street (River Road), two miles east of Shepherdstown on the Potomac River. A natural game and Indian crossing, it was used by numerous settlers moving down from the north. The most notable military crossing was made when Lee's army withdrew from the Antietam battlefield in September 1862. The Corn Exchange Regiment from Pennsylvania, sent in pursuit of Lee, suffered terrible casualties at the Battle of Cement Mill at this site. Confederate General A.P. Hill, who witnessed the battle, stated,". . . the most terrible slaughter that this war has yet witnessed. The broad surface of the Potomac was blue with the floating bodies of our foe. But few escaped to tell the tale."

THIS CROSSING OF THE POTOMAC WAS KNOWN AS BOTELER'S, BLACKFORD'S OR THE SHEPHERDSTOWN FORD. BY IT FIVE DIVISIONS OF THE ARMY OF NORTHERN VIRGINIA, COMING FROM HARPER'S FERRY, CROSSED INTO MARYLAND, SEPTEMBER 16 AND 17, 1862, AND MARCHED TO THE FIELD OF ANTIETAM. JACKSON'S AND EWELL'S DIVISIONS CROSSED THE FORD ON THE MORNING OF THE 16TH; McLAWS' AND R. H. ANDERSON'S DIVISIONS BEFORE SUNRISE ON THE 17TH, AND A. P. HILL'S DIVISION ABOUT NOON OF THE SAME DAY. DURING THE NIGHT OF THE 18TH, AND EARLY MORNING OF THE 19TH, THE ENTIRE ARMY RECROSSED FROM MARYLAND COVERED BY ARTILLERY IN POSITION ON THE VIRGINIA BLUFFS OVERLOOKING THE RIVER.

(SEPTEMBER 20, 1862)
EARLY IN THE MORNING OF SEPTEMBER 20, MOVEMENTS WERE MADE BY GEN. McCLELLAN TO ASCERTAIN THE POSITION OF THE ARMY OF NORTHERN VIRGINIA. MAJ. CHARLES S. LOVELL'S BRIGADE (1ST AND 6TH, 2D AND 10TH, THE 11TH AND THE 17TH U.S. INFANTRY) SYKES' DIVISION, FIFTH CORPS, CROSSED THE FORD AND PUSHED OUT ON THE CHARLESTOWN ROAD. BARNES' BRIGADE, MORELL'S DIVISION, WAS ORDERED TO CROSS AND MOVE ON SHEPHERDSTOWN. LOVELL HAD GONE ABOUT A MILE AND A HALF ON THE CHARLESTOWN ROAD WHEN HE MET THE CONFEDERATES IN FORCE. THE BRIGADE WAS DEPLOYED, ABOUT-FACED AND FELL BACK TO THE BLUFFS BORDERING THE RIVER AND ON EITHER SIDE OF THE CHARLESTOWN ROAD. THE 2D AND 10TH INFANTRY WERE DEPLOYED AS SKIRMISHERS IN A BELT OF WOODS ON THE LEFT FRONT. WARREN'S BRIGADE (5TH AND 10TH NEW YORK INFANTRY) SYKES' DIVISION, CROSSED AT THE FORD AND FORMED ON LOVELL'S LEFT. BARNES, BEING ORDERED BY SYKES TO FORM ON LOVELL'S RIGHT, SUSPENDED HIS MOVEMENT ON SHEPHERDSTOWN AND WENT INTO POSITION WEST OF THE MILL, 220 YARDS NORTH OF THIS POINT. LOVELL'S SKIRMISHERS AND SOME CAVALRY, WHICH HAD CROSSED AND GONE TO THE FRONT, WERE NOW PRESSED BACK BY THE ADVANCE OF A. P. HILL'S CONFEDERATE DIVISION, AND SYKES ORDERED THE ENTIRE COMMAND TO RECROSS THE POTOMAC, WHICH WAS DONE IN GOOD ORDER BY LOVELL'S AND WARREN'S BRIGADES. THE CONFEDERATE ADVANCE ON THE PART OF THE LINE HELD BY THEM BEING CHECKED BY THE FIRE OF WEED'S, RANDOL'S AND VAN REED'S BATTERIES POSTED ON THE HEIGHTS ON THE MARYLAND SIDE OF THE RIVER. BARNES' BRIGADE, THE LAST ORDERED WITHDRAWN, MET WITH GREAT LOSS AT THE MILL AND ON THE BLUFFS AND RIVER BANK BEYOND.   B. F. 9

Gen. William W. Kirkland grave, (above) in Elmwood Cemetery, Shepherdstown. Kirkland was born in North Carolina in 1833. He attended West Point, served in the U.S. Marine Corps and was elected colonel of the 21st North Carolina Infantry. He participated in many battles during the war from First Manassas to Gettysburg to the North Carolina campaign at the end of the war. He was promoted to brigadier general in August 1863. After the war he settled in Georgia but also lived in Shepherdstown for a number of years. He died in 1915 and was interned in Shepherdstown. *Courtesy Joe Ferrell*

Elmwood Cemetery, (at left and above left) in Shepherdstown. Graves of several Confederate soldiers including Henry Kyd Douglas, staff officer to Stonewall Jackson are located here.

Zion Episcopal Church and Cemetery, on East Congress Street in Charles Town. This Gothic church was built in 1851 to replace the original 1818 church on the site. During the war heavy damage was done to the interior of the building. The cemetery contains the graves of such prominent local Confederate soldiers as Lt. John Yates Beall, Capt. Daniel B. Lucas, Col. R. Preston Chew and S. Howell Brown, Gen. Robert E. Lee's cartographer. The church contains a memorial window to Col. Angus W. MacDonald. Many members of George Washington's family are also buried here.

Cameron's Depot, on state Route 51, five miles west of Charles Town. On Aug. 21, 1864, Federal forces under Gen. Philip H. Sheridan were defeated by Confederate Gen. Jubal A. Early. The fighting swept over such fine estates as Harewood, Sulgrave, Tuscawillow, Cedar Lawn and Locust Hill.

Captain John Yates Beall grave, in the Zion Episcopal graveyard, Charles Town. Beall was born in Virginia in 1835 and graduated from the University of Virginia in law. At the outbreak of the war he enlisted as a private in the Confederate Army and fought at First Manassas, where he was wounded. After recuperating, he joined the Confederate Navy as a privateer, attaining the rank of captain. He later went to Canada and was the leader of an unsuccessful attempt to free prisoners-of-war from Johnson's Island in Ohio. Trying to escape back to Canada after derailing a train near Buffalo, New York, Beall was captured by the Niagara City Police on Dec. 16, 1864. He was tried by a military commission for espionage and hanged on Governor's Island, New York City on Feb. 24, 1865, the first person to be hanged as a spy in that military district since Maj. John Andre was hanged on Oct. 2, 1780, for his part in Benedict Arnold's plot. Abraham Lincoln said of him, "There had to be an example—I had to stand firm —I can't get the distress out of mind yet." *Courtesy Joe Ferrell*

***McMurran Hall**, on King Street in Shepherdstown. It was built in 1859-60 to be used as the town hall and library but became a hospital during the war. It served as the Jefferson County Courthouse from 1866 to 1871, at which time the county seat was relocated to Charles Town. It is now owned by Shepherd College.

Kanawha County

Confederate Spy Monument, on a carriage trail opposite the Amtrak station in Charleston, below "Sunrise Mansion." During construction of Sunrise in 1905, Gov. William MacCorkle unearthed the remains of two women. He reburied them near the carriage trail. Not long after, he talked to Civil War veteran, John Slack, who declared the women had been accused of spying by the Confederate Army and had been executed after a brief "Drumhead" court-martial. Since the Confederate camp was nearby, the women were just taken up the little hollow and buried. The Governor accepted the story and had a small stone carved to acknowledge both the event and the burial. Some time later, another Civil War veteran said the story was true but that Slack had the wrong army. The Yankees had really shot the women. Finally the Governor declared that another Civil War soldier from Lincoln County had confessed on his deathbed that he had been on the Yankee firing squad and it had haunted him all his life. Historians have never been able to solve the puzzle of these women's deaths.

*Craik-Patton House (Elm Grove), at Daniel Boone Roadside Park on U.S. 60 just east of Charleston. It was built in 1834 by James Craik, grandson of George Washington's personal physician and the son of Washington's secretary. George S. Patton, a prominent Charleston lawyer and grandfather of the famous World War II general, George S. Patton III, bought the house and lived there until entering the Confederate army in 1861. Patton rose to the rank of colonel before being killed in the Battle of Winchester in 1864. It was moved in 1971 from its Charleston location to its present site and restored to its 1834 appearance by the National Society of Colonial Dames of America.

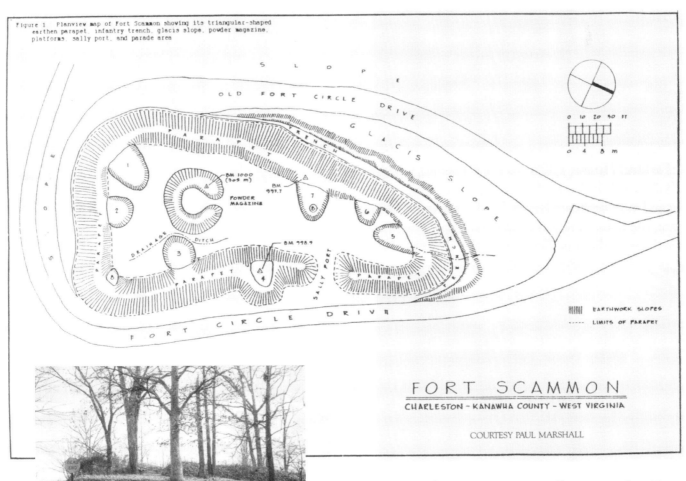

Figure 1   Planview map of Fort Scammon showing its triangular-shaped earthen parapet, infantry trench, glacis slope, powder magazine, platforms, sally port, and parade area.

FORT SCAMMON

CHARLESTON · KANAWHA COUNTY · WEST VIRGINIA

COURTESY PAUL MARSHALL

*Fort Scammon, atop Fort Hill on Charleston's south side. It was named for Col. Eliakim P. Scammon, commander of the 23rd Ohio Regiment, who was stationed in Charleston in 1863-64. The troops were actually quartered at Ferry Branch at the base of Fort Hill (now the site of gasoline storage tanks), and they built the fort more for busy work than fear of a Confederate attack because by 1863 the threat of war had largely passed by the Kanawha Valley. Restoration work and an archaeological investigation have been performed on the site in recent years.

*Littlepage Mansion, on West Washington Street at Littlepage Terrace, Charleston. Built in 1845 by Adam Littlepage, it sat at the junction of the Ripley-Ravenswood Road and the Point Pleasant Road. In July 1861 the area was the headquarters of Confederate Gen. Henry Wise, who established a camp around the house. When Mrs. Rebecca Littlepage denied him entrance, Wise threatened to blow up the residence with a cannon. Today it is used as an office by the Charleston Housing Authority.

*Holly Grove, 1710 E. Kanawha Boulevard, Charleston. The house was erected in 1815 by Daniel Ruffner. After completion of the James River and Kanawha Turnpike, the house became a popular tavern and stage stop. It was one of Charlestons finest structures at the time of the war. In 1902 the house was purchased from the Ruffner heirs and it was restored with an addition of a portico and terrace. Today the house is owned by the state and used as offices.

*McFarland House, 1310 Kanawha Boulevard, Charleston. Built in 1836 by Norris Whittaker, it is one of the valley's oldest and most significant homes. Used as a hospital during the war, it received several direct artillery hits in the 1861 campaign. The house is now headquarters for the West Virginia Humanities Council.

The grave site of noted Kanawha County resident **John P. Hale** (1824-1902), who organized an artillery battery for the Confederate Army and fought at the Battle of Scary Creek. He was a historian, physician, and businessman and a leader to move the state capitol to Charleston. He was also the mayor of Charleston in 1871.

A six pound (solid shot) **cannon ball** that struck the McFarland House during the Battle of Charleston.

Ruffner Memorial Park, (left and below) 1500 block of Kanawha Boulevard, Charleston. It was deeded to the city of Charleston by Joseph Ruffner, who bought the land from Charles Clendenin in the late 1700s. Buried here are Elizabeth, wife of Daniel Ruffner, and Joseph and Anna Ruffner. In the center of the park is a memorial to the Kanawha Riflemen, Charlestons most famous Confederate organization.

*Glenwood, 800 Orchard Street in Charleston. It was built in 1852 for James M. Laidley, a prominent early salt maker. Judge George W. Summers bought the home in 1857. Summers was a delegate from Kanawha County to the secession convention in Richmond in 1861. Summers, along with 31 other delegates from the western counties, voted against the state's withdrawal from the Union, but they were voted down. He was also a Virginia commissioner to the Washington Peace Conference in 1861. During the war he remained neutral but soldiers camped around the house. The home has been restored and is owned by the Historic Glenwood Association.

Capitol Statuary. Five statues pertaining to the Civil War have been erected on the grounds of the West Virginia State Capitol in Charleston.

a) Stonewall Jackson Statue, erected in 1910 on the grounds of the old capitol building in downtown Charleston by the United Daughters of the Confederacy. It was moved to the present building site in 1925.

b) Mountaineer Statue, erected in 1912 at the old capitol. The statue is a symbol of the men of western Virginia who formed themselves into Home Guards and responded to Lincoln's call to arms in 1861. It, too, was moved to the present capitol building site in the 1920s.

c) Union Statue, was authorized by the state legislature as a memorial "To the 32,000 soldiers, sailors and marines contributed by West Virginia to the Union-1861 to 1865."

d) Booker T. Washington Memorial, moved to the north end of the west wing in 1985 from its former location near Malden. This famous black educator lived in Malden from 1865 to 1872.

Ravenswood, on MacQueen Boulevard in St. Albans. One of the city's oldest and most elegant homes, it was built in 1833 by Francis Thompson. In 1859 James Frazier Hansford acquired the estate, and he and his wife, Anne, lived there until they died. Family tradition holds that the house was once sold, but since mortgage payments were made with Confederate money, after considerable litigation, the title reverted back to the family. It is now a private residence.

e) Abraham Lincoln Statue, dedicated on June 20, 1974 in front of the capitol, facing the Kanawha River. It was on April 20, 1863, that President Lincoln signed the proclamation creating West Virginia as the 35th state effective 60 days later on June 20, 1863.

Confederate graves, Spring Hill Cemetery in Charleston. No information is available as to when the graves were placed here. A few of them have a faint identification on their headstone. The cemetery also contains the grave of Confederate Lt. Adam B. Littlepage who was killed in Virginia in 1862.

Monument to 10 unknown Civil War soldiers at Spring Hill Cemetery, Charleston, Kanawha County. Dedicated Sept. 17, 1994.

James Clark Welch grave site, in Spring Hill Cemetery, Charleston. Welch was one of four Confederate soldiers killed at the Battle of Scary Creek. *Courtesy Gary Bays*

* **Virginia's Chapel and Slave Cemetery** (The Littie Brick Church), on U.S. 60 at Cedar Grove. The church was built in 1853 by prominent local businessman, William Tompkins, at the request of his daughter, Virginia. It was built in lieu of a trip abroad as a graduation present. During the war it served as a Confederate hospital and as a stable for Federal cavalry. After the war the Federal Government paid the church $700 for wartime damages. The church has since been restored. The slave cemetery is located behind the church.

Morgan's Plantation Kitchen, on U.S. 60 at the St. Albans Riverside Park. This small log building, which was originally located on John Morgans farm in Putnam County, was used as a hospital after the Battle of Scary Creek.

This remarkable topographical map was probably drawn by a Union army engineer in 1863 or 1864 and shows Charleston and the surrounding area. It apparently indicates every building in town at that time, the earliest map to do this. The James River and Kanawha Turnpike is shown (a) along with the turnpike to Point Pleasant (b), and the bridge site across Lovell Street (c), now Washington Street (the bridge, which is not shown, was partially destroyed in 1862). Capitol Street (d), then Cox's Lane, is definitely shown, along with Morris (e) and Bradford (f) streets, the east end of town at the time. Note the large swampy area (g) in the east end. Fort Scammon (h) is outlined, and Camp White (i) was at the bottom of Fort Hill at Ferry Branch. There is another possible fortification (j) north of town that could have been built by the Confederates. The lines at (k) are unknown. There are many other symbols shown on the map which are unknown because no legend accompanied this map.
National Archives

81

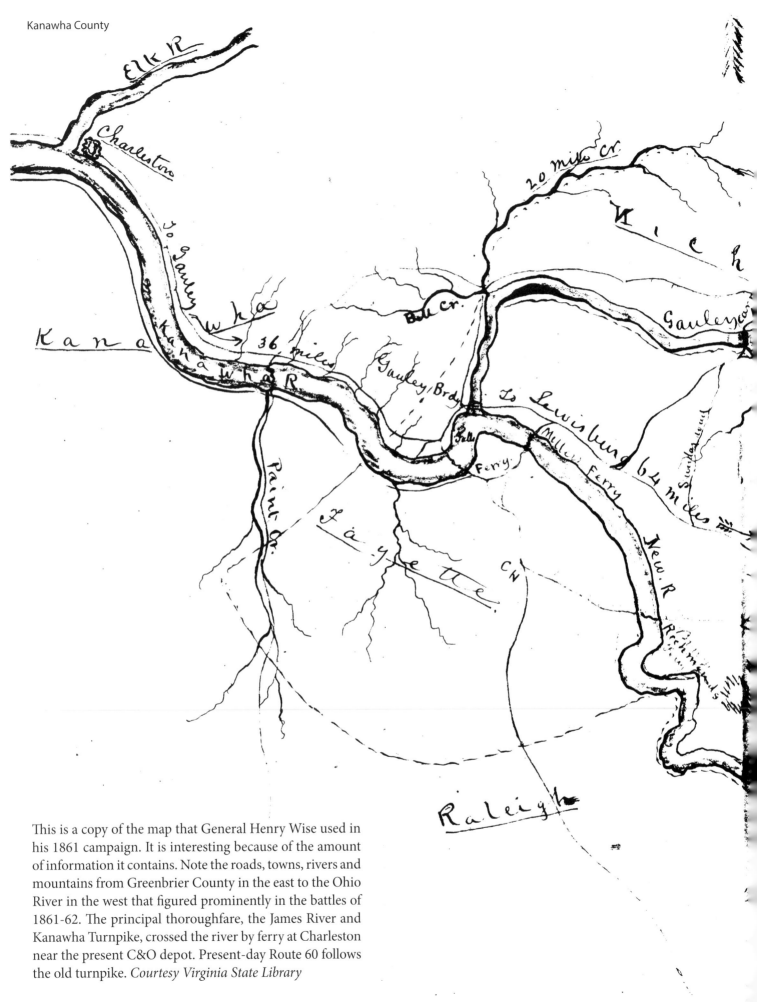

Labels on map: Elk R., Charleston, To Gauley, Kanawha, 36 miles, Kanawha R., Kanawha, Bell Cr., Gauley Brd., 20 mile cr., Rich, Gauley, To Lewisburg 64 miles, Miller Ferry, Falls Ferry, New R., Paint Cr., Fayette, Cr., Raleigh

This is a copy of the map that General Henry Wise used in his 1861 campaign. It is interesting because of the amount of information it contains. Note the roads, towns, rivers and mountains from Greenbrier County in the east to the Ohio River in the west that figured prominently in the battles of 1861-62. The principal thoroughfare, the James River and Kanawha Turnpike, crossed the river by ferry at Charleston near the present C&O depot. Present-day Route 60 follows the old turnpike. *Courtesy Virginia State Library*

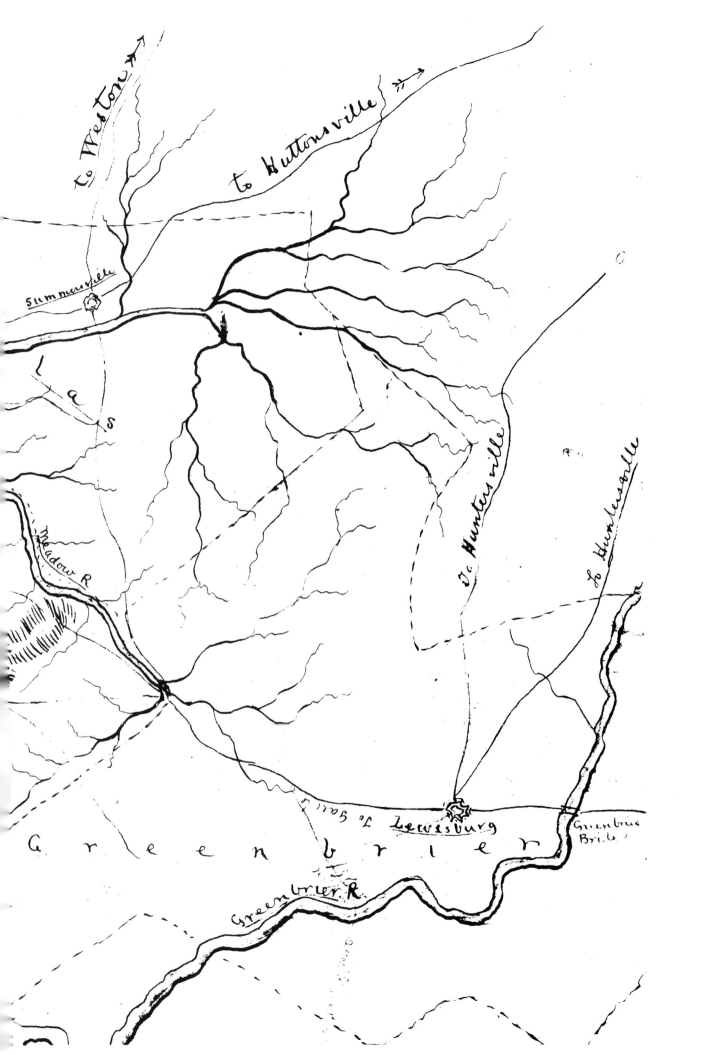

to Weston

to Huttonsville

Summersville

L
A
S

Meadow R

To Huntersville

to Huntersville

to Gauly

Lewisburg

Greenbrier
Bridge

G r e e n b r i e r

Greenbrier R.

*Cedar Grove, located in the town of Cedar Grove on the Kanawha River, east of Charleston. The house was built by William Tompkins, prominent businessman of the area, in 1844. The brother of his wife, Rachel, was the father of Gen. Ulysses S. Grant. During the war, Federal cavalry rode through Cedar Grove and threatened to burn down the Tompkins' home. Mrs. Tompkins reportedly produced a letter from General Grant promising immunity for her property. The house is still owned by a Tompkins heir.

*St. Marks Episcopal Church, 405-407 "B" Street in St. Albans. It was built in 1845. Federal troops took over the church in 1863, tore up the floorboards for firewood and used the interior as a stable. In 1915 the Federal Government made a small restitution to the congregation for the damage.

Absalom Bowen Tavern (Six-Mile House), on Tyler Mountain Road. Gen. Henry Wise's troops used this tavern as a source of drinking water in 1861. The outer walls have been stuccoed but the house retains much of its pre-Civil War look. On the nearby Big Tyler Mountain overlooking the tavern, was a Confederate outpost which was hastily abandoned in the summer of 1861. It is now a private residence. *Courtesy Terry Lowry*

*Felix Hansford House, at the mouth of Paint Creek, just off state Route 61 at Hansford. The house was built in 1826 and armies of both sides passed by during the war. Confederate troops rested here on their retreat from the Kanawha Valley in July 1861. The house is currently in very poor condition.

An early, post-war view of the Hansford house. *Courtesy Paul Marshall*

A sketch of the **covered bridge over Coal River** at what is now Main Street in St. Albans as it appeared in 1861. The bridge was burned by Confederate troops as they retreated from the Kanawha Valley in 1861. John N. Overshiner, a Federal soldier from Coalsmouth (now St. Albans), drew this from memory. *Courtesy William Wintz*

Confederate Civil War graves, in Rust Cemetery overlooking the mouth of Coal River in St. Albans. Buried here are Pvt. James W. Rust, who served in Co. A, 22nd Virginia Infantry Regiment and fell at the Battle of Fayetteville, Sept. 10, 1862, and Pvt. Henry Gregory also in Co. A, who was killed Aug. 26, 1863 at the Battle of White Sulphur Springs. *Courtesy William Wintz*

*****Dutch Hollow Wine Cellars,** on Dutch Hollow Road in Dunbar. A remnant of the once-thriving wine industry in the Kanawha Valley. Thomas Friend operated the business until the Civil War stopped all wine production. Production was attempted again after the war but the effort wasn't successful. The cellars have been restored and are part of a city park.

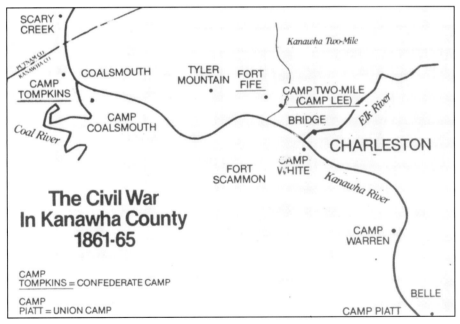

This is thought to be the earliest known photograph taken in the **Charleston** area (above). Several historians have placed this in 1863 or 1864. The men are lined up along Front Street (Kanawha Boulevard) outfitted in some type of fraternal regalia. A few Union soldiers can be picked out in the crowd. It is not known what the occasion was. The three-story building is the Bank of the West at the corner of Front and Summers streets. E.T. Moore, who moved to Charleston from Gallipolis, Ohio, sometime during the Civil War, has his printing business sign displayed and apparently is painting a large sign with his name on it (The E has already been done). By June 1864, Moore was joined by his brother S. Spencer Moore. The business was known as Moore & Brother, Publishers. The building on the extreme right is the Laidley Drug Store with a statue of the Goddess of Health, Hygeia, and the word OIL on the column. *Courtesy Dave Moore*

Lewis County

Fort Pickens, on county Route 50 at Duffy, two miles east of Ireland on U.S. 19. Co. A, 10th West Virginia Volunteer Infantry built the fort in 1861-62. It burned in 1864.

Jackson's Mill, on county Route 12, three miles north of Weston. The mill was built in 1837 on the farm of Col. Edward Jackson, grandfather of Gen. Thomas Jonathan (Stonewall) Jackson. Young Jackson lived here from 1830 to 1842, leaving his birthplace in Clarksburg after his widowed mother remarried.

Young Tom was six when he came to the farm with his sister, Laura. He performed his share of the lighter chores,

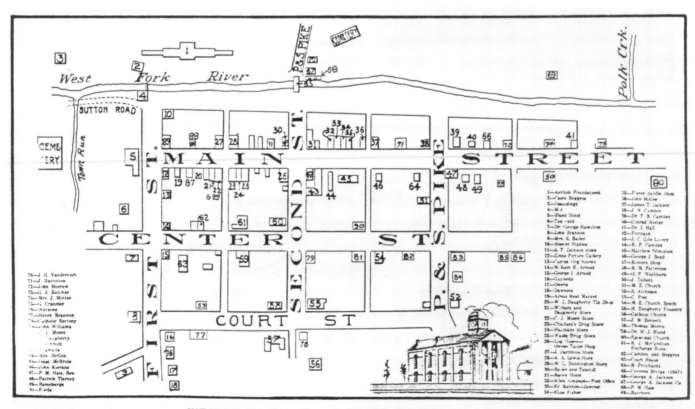

WESTON IN 1860, (insert) COURT HOUSE 1856-7-1886

and as he grew older, joined the slaves and hired men in the forest felling trees for his grandfather's sawmill. Nervous indigestion, which was to trouble him all his life, made him seek eagerly for outdoor activity. He worked under the millers in the gristmill, broke flax with a flail, and tended sheep; he went fishing, coon-hunting, and boating on the West Fork River, attended a country school, and engaged in fisticuffs with his schoolmates. His sketchy schooling aroused in him a desire for greater learning, so he struck a bargain with a slave; the slave was to furnish pine knots to provide light so that Jackson could study at night; in return, the boy promised to teach the slave to read and write. The slave learned well and later escaped by the Underground Railroad to Canada.

In 1837 Jackson was employed in the construction of the Parkersburg and Staunton Turnpike, and in these years he walked three miles each Sunday to hear a sermon. Impressed by his serious character and desire for learning, Col. Alexander Scott Withers, a justice of the peace, secured an appointment for Jackson as a constable in 1841, a position of dignity and authority in those days. The following year he passed the required examinations and enrolled in the U.S. Military Academy at West Point.

Jackson's boyhood here at the Mills was probably the happiest period of his life, and he often referred to the memories of his youth; a canoe made from a hollowed tree trunk, associated with so many of his boyish escapades, is believed to have been in his mind when he spoke these last words as he lay dying: "Let us cross over the river and rest in the shade of the trees."

The site is now owned by West Virginia University and is the state 4-H camp.

Jackson's Mill in the late 1800s. Jackson's home was built about 1837. The site is now a museum with one restored and one reconstructed mill on the property.

McWhorter Cabin, on the site of the original Jackson home at Jackson's Mill. Built about 1793 at Jane Lew by Henry McWhorter, a Revolutionary War soldier, the log house was moved to Jackson's Mill in 1927.

Gen. Joseph A.J. Lightburn grave The grave of Federal Gen. Joseph A.J. Lightburn is located in the Broad Run Baptist Church cemetery at Lightburn on county Route 8, 3.3 miles west of Jane Lew. Lightburn was born in 1824 in Pennsylvania. He moved to the Broad Run, West Fork River area of Lewis County in 1841. He and his father operated a grist mill on the West Fork River. He served in the Mexican War along with his good friend Thomas J. Jackson. In 1859 Lightburn became a Baptist preacher and in 1861 attended the state convention in Wheeling. He was appointed colonel of the 4th West Virginia Regiment in August 1861 and was best known in West Virginia for his command of forces in the Kanawha Valley and his retreat from the valley in September 1862. The rest of the war he spent in the Vicksburg area and in Georgia except the last year, which he spent in West Virginia and Maryland. After the war he served in the West Virginia Legislature, continued his ministry work and taught school. He died in 1901. *Courtesy Joe Ferrell*

*Former Weston State Hospital, in Weston, county seat of Lewis County. In 1859 the town was chosen as the site for the Trans-Allegheny Lunatic Asylum. Located on the southern edge of town, it is the oldest public institution in the state. The three one-story wings were completed in 1864, the main building in 1880. There have been many additions and reconstructions through the years. It is said to be the largest hand-cut stone structure in the country. It was one of the few tangible properties West Virginia had to show for the $13 million debt owed Virginia after the Civil War. The center section is now open for tours six days a week and restoration continues on the building.

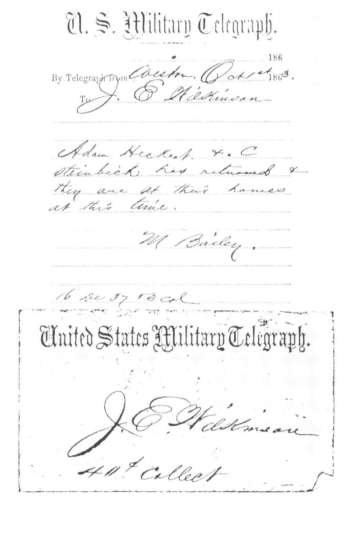

Lincoln County

Griffithsville Skirmish site, on state Route 3, just west of Griffithsville. This engagement took place in the summer of 1863. Advancing Federal forces, commanded by Maj. John S. Witcher, were halted and forced to retreat by Confederate troops under the command of Capt. Peter Carpenter.

Logan County

*Hatfield Cemetery,** on U.S. 119 near Sarah Ann. This cemetery contains the graves of many of the Hatfield clan, who participated in the famous Hatfield-McCoy feud that raged along the West Virginia-Kentucky border between 1882-1886. The grave of clan leader, "Devil Anse" Hatfield, who served in the Confederate army as a lieutenant in the 45th Battalion of Virginia Infantry and later as a captain of the local home guard, is marked by a life-size statue of Italian Carrara marble.

Marion County

*Barracksville Covered Bridge, county Route 21 over Buffalo Creek at Barracksville. Built in 1853 by famed bridge builder Lemuel Chenoweth, it is an extremely well-preserved example of a modified Burr-Truss system. It is 148 feet long and is considered to be the most historically intact of West Virginia's covered bridges. Local residents saved it from destruction by pleading with Confederate Gen. William E. Jones who passed here on his raid in April 1863. It has been completely restored.

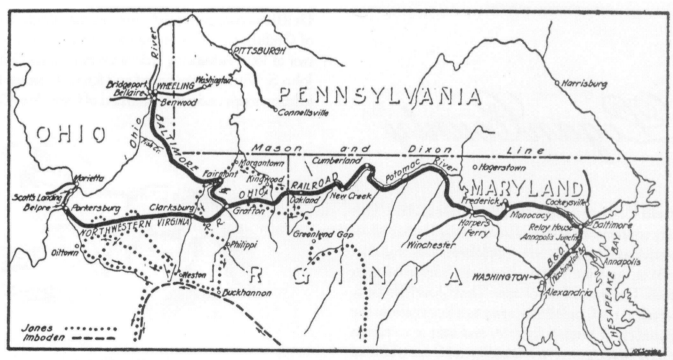

THE JONES-IMBODEN RAID (1863)

*Job Prickett House, located off I-79 (Exit 139), five miles north of Fairmont on county Route 73/3 at Pricketts Fort State Park. The house was built by Job H. Prickett, great-grandson of Capt. Jacob Prickett, the man for whom Pricketts Fort was named. Work was started on the house in 1859 and continued for the next several years. During this time Job Prickett and his wife Louisa and their children had been living in a log house directly behind the brick house under construction. The house is a unique example of a mid-19th century farm house. Family tradition states that the bricks used to build the house were made on site with clay dug from the area.

Although the house was constructed in the traditional folk-style architecture, it has several unusual features that make it unique. One such feature is the interesting dentil work along the cornice line just below the roof. Also of interest is the cut stone foundation. Stone with this quality cutting and dressing was very unusual for a rural, private dwelling during this period.

Inside the house, now a museum, authentically garbed interpreters stand ready to answer questions about the house, its inhabitants, and Civil War era farm life.

Site of Pierpont House, on the northeast corner of Pierpont Avenue and Quincy Street in Fairmont. This site is the former home of Gov. Francis H. Pierpont, who was elected governor of the Restored Government of Virginia at the second Wheeling Convention. After the state was admitted to the Union, he moved the government to Alexandria, Virginia, until the end of the war. Confederate Gen. William E. Jones ransacked the house on his famous raid through town on April 29, 1863. The house was razed in 1934.

Pierpont's grave, in Woodlawn Cemetery in Fairmont. Gov. Francis H. Pierpont, who was born in Monongalia County in 1814, died in 1899 and was buried in Woodlawn Cemetery. His statue was placed in the Capitol Building in Washington, D.C. To the right of Pierpont's grave is that of his wife, Julia Augusta Robertson Pierpont. Behind the graves are members of the West Virginia Re-enactors Association, Inc.

Mason County

*Powell-Redmond House, 23 Columbia Street, Clifton. Overlooking the Ohio River, this beautiful Italianate residence was built by and was the home of Federal Maj. Gen. William H. Powell. It is now a private residence.

Gen. John McCausland House, on state Route 35 near Pliny. Constructed in 1885, this unique stone house with its original octagonal belvedere, or turret, was the home of Confederate Gen. John McCausland. McCausland fought in many engagements in West Virginia and was famous for his burning of Chambersburg, Pa. in 1864. When he died in 1927, he was the next-to-last Confederate general officer.

Gen. John McCausland's grave, located near Henderson in the Smith graveyard on a hill overlooking the Ohio River. The gravesite is isolated and can only be seen by walking up the hill. The obelisk-type monument is a marker for one of the oldest graves of the Smith family. A new marker simply states: "John McCausland 1836-1927." *Courtesy Joe Ferrell*

Gen. McCausland and his daughter, Charlotte. *Courtesy Terry Lowry*

Mercer County

*Col. William Henderson French House, off state Route 20 near Athens. This is one of the finest antebellum structures in this part of the state and in all probability the oldest continuously inhabited house in Mercer County. It was constructed in 1855 as a residence for William Henderson French, a prominent local politician and colonel in the Confederate Army who commanded the 17th Regiment of Virginia Cavalry, participating in the Gettysburg campaign and in numerous campaigns in southwestern Virginia. It is now a private residence.

McNutt House, corner of Honaker Avenue and North Walker Street in Princeton. The house was set on fire when retreating Confederate forces burned Princeton on May 1, 1862. Federal troops put out the fire and made the house their headquarters. Only two houses were left standing in the Mercer County seat. Among the Federal force were two future U.S. presidents, Rutherford B. Hayes and William McKinley. The house is now a private residence.

Camp Jones Marker, on U.S. 19, seven-tenths of a mile south of I-77 bridge over U.S. 19.

CAMP JONES

Here in 1862 was stationed the 23rd Ohio Regt., U.S.A. Encamped were Gen. J. D. Cox, Maj. R. B. Hayes and Sergt. William McKinley. All became governors of Ohio; Hayes and McKinley became Presidents of the United States.

Mineral County

Fort Fuller, a strong Federal fort during the war, stood where the Administration Building at Potomac State College in Keyser now stands. Keyser was a supply point and battleground for both Federal and Confederate forces. Between 1861 and 1865 the town was captured and recaptured 14 times. Both sides made determined fights to hold the railroad, and when Confederates finally lost control they destroyed it. In November 1864, General T.L. Rosser with 2,000 Confederate soldiers surprised the 800 Federals garrisoning Fort Fuller and took the town, capturing large stores of munitions and most of the Federal force. Supply houses were burned; most of the business section and miles of railroad track were destroyed. The Confederates were soon routed by General Kelley's army, which remained in the valley to protect the railroad.

Nancy Hanks Monument, on county Route 6/2. Follow the signs from Ridgeville for several miles to this remote spot south of Antioch. The mother of Abraham Lincoln was supposedly born at this site in the 1780s. The monument marks the cabin site and a replica cabin is nearby. The Nancy Hanks Commission erected the monument in September 1929 although at the time the Lincoln National Life Foundation stated: "There is not one shred of evidence of documentary nature that implies Nancy Hanks ever lived within several hundred miles of the spot."

VANDIVER-TROUT-CLAUSE HOUSE
Located on a 1766 Fairfax grant and site of a former blockhouse. Built by John Vandiver in early 19th century; soon operated as an ordinary. Henry Trout purchased the house in 1869, repairing damage done during the Civil War. In the latter half of the century the house was also a post office and polling place. In 1904 the property was sold to Henry Clause, the inn's last proprietor.

Vandiver-Trout-Clause House, at Ridgeville on U.S. 50/220.

KEYSER

Between 1861-1865, Keyser then New Creek, was sought by the North and South. It changed hands fourteen times. Fort Fuller, where Potomac State College stands, was supported by a series of forts girding the town.

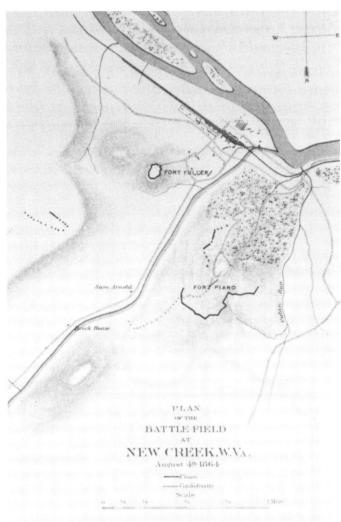

PLAN
OF THE
BATTLE FIELD
AT
NEW CREEK, W.VA.
August 4th 1864

Union
Confederate
Scale

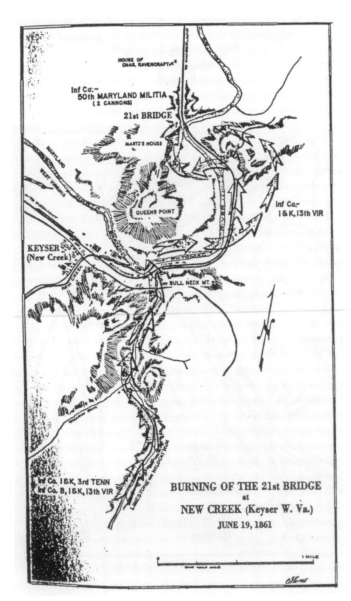

HOUSE OF CHAS. RAVENCRAFT

Inf Co:- 50th MARYLAND MILITIA (2 CANNONS)

21st BRIDGE

MARTZ'S HOUSE

MARYLAND

WEST VIRGINIA

QUEENS POINT

Inf Co:- I & K, 13th VIR

KEYSER (New Creek)

BULL NECK MT.

Inf Co. I & K, 3rd TENN
Inf Co. B, I & K, 13th VIR

BURNING OF THE 21st BRIDGE
at
NEW CREEK (Keyser W. Va.)
JUNE 19, 1861

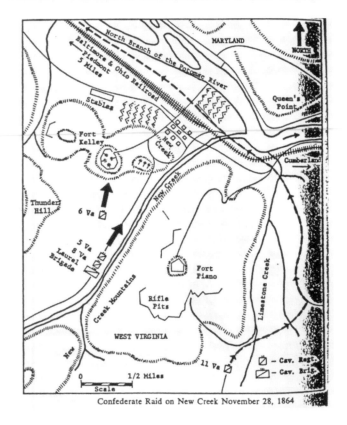

Confederate Raid on New Creek November 28, 1864

Monroe County

*Gen. John Echols Home, on Elmwood and 2nd Avenue in Union. It was built between 1845 and 1848 and was owned by General Echols for 20 years. It is one of the oldest and best-preserved landmarks of the pre-Civil War period in the county. Echols organized the Monroe Guards before the war and entered the Confederate army as a lieutenant colonel of the 27th Virginia Infantry. He was promoted to brigadier general in 1862 and major general in 1865. His military career was mostly spent in West Virginia and southwest Virginia including command of the Confederate army at Droop Mountain. He lived in Staunton, Virginia from 1865 until his death in 1896. He was instrumental in promoting the building of the Chesapeake and Ohio Railway and through the years, was a lawyer, educator and statesman.

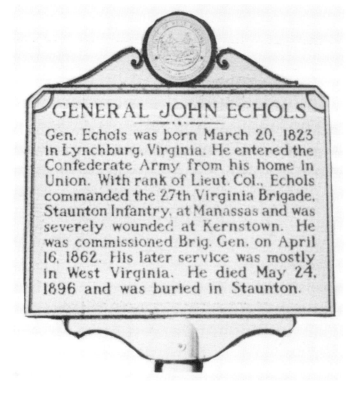

GENERAL JOHN ECHOLS

Gen. Echols was born March 20, 1823 in Lynchburg, Virginia. He entered the Confederate Army from his home in Union. With rank of Lieut. Col., Echols commanded the 27th Virginia Brigade, Staunton Infantry, at Manassas and was severely wounded at Kernstown. He was commissioned Brig. Gen. on April 16, 1862. His later service was mostly in West Virginia. He died May 24, 1896 and was buried in Staunton.

SALTPETER CAVES

The large rooms of these caves have high vaults and are easily accessible from the outside and are dry under foot. They were owned by John Maddy in 1804. He sold them to Jacob and John Mann who manufactured saltpeter here for several years. The caves were used for the same purpose during Civil War. Old wooden hoppers still stand and mule tracks can yet be seen on the long walkways where the wagons used to run.

*Elmwood (Hugh Caperton House), on U.S. 219 on the north end of Union. This stately mansion was built in 1835 of native materials. It was the home of merchant and Congressman Hugh Caperton and later his son, Alan T., who served in both the Confederate and United States Senate. Henry Clay was such a frequent visitor to the home that a bedroom is named the "Henry Clay Room." It is now a private residence.

Greenville Saltpeter Cave, off county Route 23/4, one and one-half miles northeast of Greenville. A limestone cave, said to be the largest complex in West Virginia, made up of six large openings and over two and one-half miles of explored interconnected passages, old roadways, mule tracks and hoppers from the saltpeter manufacturing during the Civil War.

CIVIL WAR MONUMENT

On Aug. 21, 1901 this 20 ft. monument with 6 ft. statue depicting typical Confederate soldier was dedicated to the Monroe County men who served the lost cause. Hinton Marble Works produced the Italian marble statue, standing on granite pedestal placed on native blue limestone. Site selected in anticipation of Union's growth. Dedication crowd of 10,000 heard speech of Gen. John Echols.

This marker is incorrect. Echols died in 1896, so he couldn't have dedicated the monument in 1901.

Civil War Monument, in a field on the north end of Union, off U.S. 219 and state Route 3, just past the Presbyterian Church. Why is the monument located in a field instead of on a street in town? Two possible theories have been put forward: One is that the town was expected to grow in that direction, northward, eventually to encompass the monument, which would be the focus of a park. The other involves the nature of life in West Virginia during and after the war. When the monument was built, could local government have been controlled by those who deemed a Confederate monument inappropriate for an in-town site? No one seems to know.

***Red Sulphur Springs,** on state Route 12 in the western end of the county. This was the site of a popular pre-war resort established in 1835, and during the war the buildings were used as a Confederate hospital. The property was bought by Levi P. Morton, vice-president under President Benjamin Harrison, who offered the springs to the state in 1906 as a site for a tuberculosis sanatorium. The state turned him down and all the buildings were demolished. Only the spring enclosure in a pasture is left. There are several Confederate graves in the vicinity.

The elegant **Erskine house**, built in 1836, was one of the two large hotel buildings standing during the war.

*Salt Sulphur Springs, (above) on U.S. 219, two miles south of Union. This large, famous health resort is remarkably well-preserved. It was opened in the 1820s and was visited by Henry Clay, John C. Calhoun, and presidents James Monroe and Martin Van Buren. During the war it was a major rest and staging area, mainly for Confederate troops. The large hotel building with a white-columned portico is now a private residence. There are Confederate graves in the vicinity.

Ruins of the Erskine House.

*__Old Sweet Springs__, at the junction of state Routes 3 and 311. One of Americas oldest mineral water resorts, reflecting the vacationing aspects of the country's fashionable society of more than a century ago. The resort dates from the 18th century, and the main building was constructed in 1833, said to be based on a design by Thomas Jefferson (though this is not proved). The site was a rest area for troops during the war. It is named in honor of Andrew S. Rowan, who carried the famous "Message to Garcia" during the Spanish-American War.

The swimming pool and baths (photo, center).

Original 1830s brick cottages (right).

Morgan County

Paw Paw, on state Route 9 along the Potomac River.

*****Berkeley Springs**, at the junction of U.S. 522 and state Route 9. The county seat of Morgan County was a famous health resort established as a town called Bath in 1776. The area was not the scene of any major action during the war but underwent a succession of captures and recaptures with much destruction of property. The resort was not to regain its popularity after the war.

The Pavillion Hotel (bottom left) at Berkeley Springs was built in the 1840s and burned down in 1898.

Stonewall Jackson Hill, on U.S. 522, south of the Potomac River Bridge. From this point, Jackson shelled Hancock, Maryland, on Jan. 5, 1862. After destroying supplies and the Baltimore & Ohio Railroad track and bridge over the Great Cacapon, he marched his army of 8,500 men to Romney and captured it on January 14.

Nicholas County

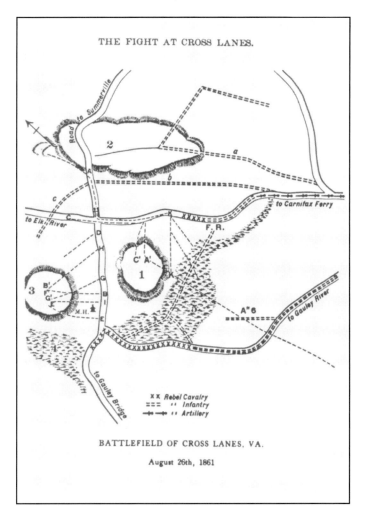

THE FIGHT AT CROSS LANES.

BATTLEFIELD OF CROSS LANES, VA.

August 26th, 1861

XX *Rebel Cavalry*
=== " *Infantry*
→ " *Artillery*

Battle of Cross Lanes site, at Kesslers Cross Lanes at the junction of state Route 129 and county Route 9 just north of the Carnifex Ferry Battlefield site. This was the site of a battle between Colonel E.B. Tyler's 7th Regiment of Ohio Volunteer Infantry and Gen. John B. Floyd's Confederate force on Aug. 26, 1861. The Confederates attacked about 5:00 a.m. while the Federals were preparing breakfast. The battle lasted less than an hour and the Federals were completely routed with losses of two killed, 29 wounded and 110 taken prisoner. Confederate losses were five killed and 15 wounded. Federal troops were billeted at the Vaughan House before the battle and the home served as a hospital afterward. Fighting occurred around the site of the present day Zoar Church.

Cross Lanes Battlefield site. *Courtesy Terry Lowry*

The Vaughan House shown in a state of neglect and decay. It is now gone. *Courtesy Gary Bays*

The Vaughan House, which was used as a Federal headquarters and hospital during the war, as it appeared in 1936. *Mudd Library, Oberlin College*

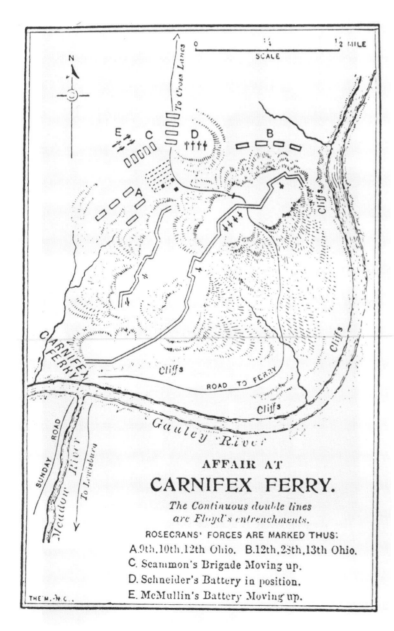

AFFAIR AT
CARNIFEX FERRY.
*The Continuous double lines
are Floyd's entrenchments.*
ROSECRANS' FORCES ARE MARKED THUS:
A. 9th, 10th, 12th Ohio. B. 12th, 23th, 13th Ohio.
C. Scammon's Brigade Moving up.
D. Schneider's Battery in position.
E. McMullin's Battery Moving up.

*Carnifex Ferry Battlefield State Park, on county Route 23 just south of state Route 129, one mile east of the Summersville Dam. The most developed of the state's two Civil War Battlefield state parks was the scene of a large battle between Confederate forces under Gen. John B. Floyd and Federal forces under Gen. William S. Rosecrans on Sept. 10, 1861. The Confederate defeat opened up this section of the state for an extended period of Federal control.

The Patteson House is on the original battlefield. It was used as a hospital after the battle and is now a small museum.

Patteson Trail, showing original foxholes.

Carnifex Ferry Battlefield State Park in the in the 1930s. *W.Va. Dept. of Culture & History*

Gen. William S. Rosecrans

Gen. John B. Floyd

Young Monument, on Young Monument Road just off U.S. 19, south of Birch River. Henry Young, who is buried here, was a Confederate militiaman. He was shot by Federal troops on Powell Mountain on Sept. 8, 1861 when he mistook them for Confederates. His son placed a monument at his gravesite which was moved to make way for a realigned U.S. 19.

Ohio County

West Virginia's First Capitol Building, at the corner of Eoff and Fifteenth streets in Wheeling. Erected in 1858, this building housed the Linsly Institute whose charter goes back to 1814 when it was known as the Lancastrian Academy. The academy was the first chartered school for free education in a slave state. The building was used as the capitol from June 20, 1863 to April 1, 1870, in spite of Governor Boreman's repeated requests for a permanent site. The structure has been altered considerably. *Courtesy Schneider Studios, Wheeling*

*****West Virginia Independence Hall**, 1524 Market Street, Wheeling, built in 1859 to serve as the U.S. Customhouse. The Second Wheeling Convention, which drew up West Virginia's Declaration of Independence from Virginia in 1861, was held here, and the building not only gave birth to the state of West Virginia but was the capitol of the Restored Government of Virginia until 1863. During the war the building also served as an arsenal, and after the war citizens were required to swear anew their allegiance to the Union here. The building has been restored and is a museum operated by the West Virginia Department of Culture & History. It is now a National Historic Landmark. *W.Va. Dept. of Culture & History*

Linsly Institute as it looked during the Civil War. The school moved out of this building in 1925. *W.Va. Dept. of Culture & History*

Stone Front, 1406 Main Street. The two sections were built before and after June 20, 1863.

FRANK LESLIE'S ILLUSTRATED NEWSPAPER.

FRANK LESLIE, Editor and Publisher.

NEW YORK, SEPTEMBER 7, 1861.

All Communications, Books for Review, &c., must be addressed to FRANK LESLIE, 19 City Hall Square, New York.

TERMS FOR THIS PAPER.

One Copy	17 weeks	$ 1
One do.	1 year	$ 5
Two do.	1 year	$ 5
Or One Copy	2 years	$ 5
Three Copies	1 year	$ 6
Five do.	1 year (to one address)	$10

And an extra Copy to the person sending a Club of Five. Every additional subscription, $2.

The State of Kanawha.

CONTRARY to the best judgment of most, but in consonance with the wishes of many, the Western Virginia State Convention, by a vote of 50 to 28, passed an ordinance on the 20th of August, subject, however, to popular ratification, establishing 39 of the western counties of Virginia as an independent commonwealth, to be known as the State of Kanawha. These counties, all of which were represented in the Convention, lie to the westward of the main chain of the Alleghanies, embracing that anomalous district projecting up between the Ohio River and Pennsylvania, and known as the "Pan Handle," and extending downward to about latitude 37 deg. 20 min. Only unmistakable Union counties are embraced in the new State, although provision is made in the ordinance for receiving such other counties as may vote to be included. It should be promised that for various reasons, one of which was the exclusion of slaves under a certain age from taxation, free Western Virginia has several times attempted to sever her connection from Eastern or slaveholding Virginia. Once, if we mistake not, an act for separation came within one vote of being carried—John Letcher, the present rebel Governor of Virginia, supporting the measure.

The motives for separation, therefore, have not arisen altogether from present complications. They have nevertheless been patent and conclusive, viewed from the Western Virginian standpoint. In the first place, the counties composing the new State embrace a rich lumber, mineral and grazing district, in parts well adapted

for the cultivation of cereals. It nowhere produces the tropical or semi-tropical staples, for the successful cultivation of which servile labor is deemed requisite. The 39 counties composing the new State have a total population, according to the census of 1860, of 281,786 souls, of which less than 8,000 are slaves. The country is therefore, practically, a free country, and as such opposed to the Secession heresy. The total population of Virginia, under the census referred to, was 1,593,199, including 495,826 slaves, leaving a white population of 1,097,373. So that in losing the population of the new State, amounting to 281,986, Virginia is shorn of about one-fourth of her white inhabitants. It is well known that there are at least 20 other counties, embracing nearly the whole of Middle Virginia, or the valley of Virginia, which would attach themselves to the new State if circumstances enabled them to give a free expression of opinion. Indeed, more than half of Virginia is regard as "Union" against "Secession." As it now stands organized (and in recognizing the new State we bow to the necessities of the case), the new commonwealth of Kanawha is one of the richest in resources of the whole Union, and in the decade between 1850 and 1860 increased more rapidly in population and wealth than any other equal extent of territory in the slave States. It abounds in minerals, coal, iron, salt and mineral oil, and with its agricultural resources possesses all the natural elements of wealth, besides the inestimable blessing of free labor. It cannot fail to become rich and powerful. It is, moreover, a region of rivers and mountains, amongst which Liberty loves to dwell, and where the strong right arms of men hew out the pillars which support the temple of Freedom.

The wisdom of the present movement, in a technical, perhaps in a political sense, fails to commend itself to the popular judgment. It, in some sort, recognises the right of Secession, which the Government of the United States, anxious to conserve the forms of legality, rigidly denies. That Government at once accepted Governor Pierpont as the *de facto* and *de jure* Governor of Virginia, in place of John Letcher, on the ground that the latter had undertaken to perform acts not sanctioned by the letter or spirit of the Constitution and laws of the State, and had forfeited, in consequence, any claim on the loyalty of the commonwealth. It is no doubt sound policy in the Federal Government thus to recognize the action of the loyal men in the several States, as the nucleus for their reorganization. It is easy to see how every State, with the possible exception of South Carolina, might thus regularly, and with all the sanction of form, be brought back into the Union. With the advance of the Federal arms, the present suppressed Union sentiment in every State might find safe expression—all that is requisite to prove that Secession and its attendant ills are the work of conspirators, and of a traitorous minority.

The action of the State Convention of Virginia, therefore, cannot fail to be embarrassing to the programme of the Government for restoring the Union. But the results achieved are nevertheless such as would have followed on any plan of reorganizing the country. Neither in sympathy nor interest is Western Virginia allied to Eastern Virginia. The social organization of its people, their interests and sentiments, are different and irreconcilable, and a separation now only anticipates a result sure to follow in the course of time, and which probably the present is the best time for bringing about. The legal adviser of the Government, the Attorney-General, pronounces against the action of the Convention as "an original, independent act of revolution," and advises an adherence to legal formulas "as dictated by the plainest teachings of prudence." But the political Saurians who compose the *personnel* of the actual Government do not recognize the fact that we are in a state of revolution, earnest, downright and vital, involving not only the national integrity, but every princi-

vital, involving not only the national integrity, but every principle of popular government, and that mere formulas will not save us. We must recognize, as the Wheeling Convention has done, the inexorable logic of facts. The Legislature assembled at Wheeling we had admitted to be the Legislature of Virginia—at any rate we have accepted United States Senators chosen by it as Senators of the United States duly elected. If that Legislature, therefore, approves the act of the Convention, and it is afterwards approved by Congress (and of the approval of both bodies there can be no doubt), then all the requirements of the Constitution as to the division and admission of States will be fulfilled. We welcome the State of Kanawha into the national galaxy! May her star be "fixed" and its light steady.

Those of our readers who are statistically inclined will find material for preservation in the following table, showing the population by counties (according to the census of 1860), of this new State of Kanawha:

Logan county	4,538	Barbour	8,959
Wyoming	2,865	Upshur	7,292
Raleigh	3,367	Harrison	13,790
Fayette	5,997	Lewis	7,999
Nicholas	4,626	Braxton	4,992
Webster	1,555	Clay	1,787
Randolph	4,990	Kanawha	14,575
Tucker	1,428	Boone	4,840
Preston	13,312	Wayne	6,747
Monongalia	13,048	Cabell	8,020
Marion	12,721	Putnam	6,301
Taylor	7,463	Mason	9,195
Jackson	8,306	Wood	11,046
Roanoke	8,048	Pleasants	2,945
Calhoun	3,502	Tyler	6,517
Wirt	3,751	Doddridge	5,203
Gilmer	3,759	Wetzel	6,703
Ritchie	6,847	Marshall	13,001
Ohio	22,422	Hancock	4,445
Brooke	5,494		
Total population			281,786

Gen. Jesse Lee Reno Memorial, at Wheeling Park on U.S. 40, Wheeling. Reno was a West Virginia general who was killed at the Battle of South Mountain in 1862.

Pendleton County

*McCoy House, on Main Street in Franklin. The house was constructed by William McCoy with slave labor. McCoy was an attorney and large land owner in Pendleton County and managed the affairs of his uncle, Gen. William McCoy, who served in Congress for 33 years and was chairman of the Ways and Means Committee. Work was begun on the house in 1848 and it was completed several years later. During the Civil War, Union forces under General R.C. Schenck used the house as their communications center prior to and during the Battle of McDowell which was fought May 8, 1862. The house is presently owned by the Pendleton County Commission.

Trout Rock Fort, on U.S. 220 at Trout Rock, four miles south of Franklin. This site marks the end of Stonewall Jackson's pursuit of the Federals on May 12, 1862 after the Battle of McDowell on May 8. Gunpowder was made here using saltpeter from a nearby cave.

Smoke Hole Caves, at the junction of U.S. 220 and state Route 2, one mile north of the Smoke Hole Road. Big Cave and Old Mines Cave were sites for saltpeter manufacture during the war.

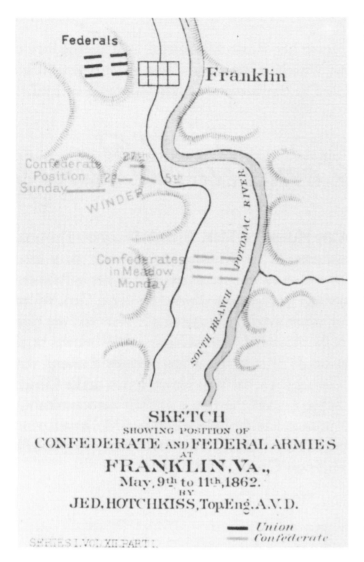

SKETCH
SHOWING POSITION OF
CONFEDERATE AND FEDERAL ARMIES
AT
FRANKLIN, VA.,
May, 9th to 11th, 1862.
BY
JED. HOTCHKISS, Top. Eng., A.V.D.

― Union
― Confederate

SERIES I, VOL. XII, PART I.

Pocahontas County

*Top of Allegheny, a remote site, just off U.S. 250 near the Virginia border. This site straddles the old Parkersburg and Staunton Turnpike and was a campground for Confederate troops in the winter of 1861-62. At an elevation of 4,250 feet, it was the highest winter campground of the war. Federal Gen. Robert Milroy marched through Camp Bartow and on Dec. 13, 1861, attacked the entrenched Confederates. He was repulsed with a loss of 137 wounded and killed. More than 4,200 feet of well-preserved trenches, gun emplacements and cabin sites are visible. The site is now partially owned and preserved by the U.S. Forest Service.

Trenches and cabin sites with the old Parkersburg and Staunton Turnpike in the distance.

The largest **gun emplacement** in the center of the old fort.

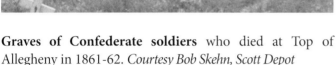

Graves of Confederate soldiers who died at Top of Allegheny in 1861-62. *Courtesy Bob Skehn, Scott Depot*

*****Traveller's Repose**, at the junction of U.S. 250 and state Route 28 at Bartow. This house was built in 1866 to replace one burned during the war. The original house contained 22 rooms and was the first overnight stage stop west of the Allegheny Mountains as well as the first county post office (1814). The site was midway between Staunton and Parkersburg. It is now a private residence.

*****Camp Bartow**, (right and below) in the vicinity of Traveller's Repose. The camp was engineered by Captain Barteau of the 3rd Arkansas Regiment and named for him. Trenches can be traced around the surrounding hills. Here at the Battle of the Greenbrier River on Oct. 3, 1861. Gen. John J. Reynolds, in command of Federal forces in the Cheat Mountain area, sent his troops to dislodge the Confederates guarding the Parkersburg and Staunton Turnpike. Although he had a superior force, the Confederates had a better position, and upon seeing reinforcements coming down the turnpike from Camp Allegheny, Reynolds broke off the engagement and returned to Cheat Mountain.

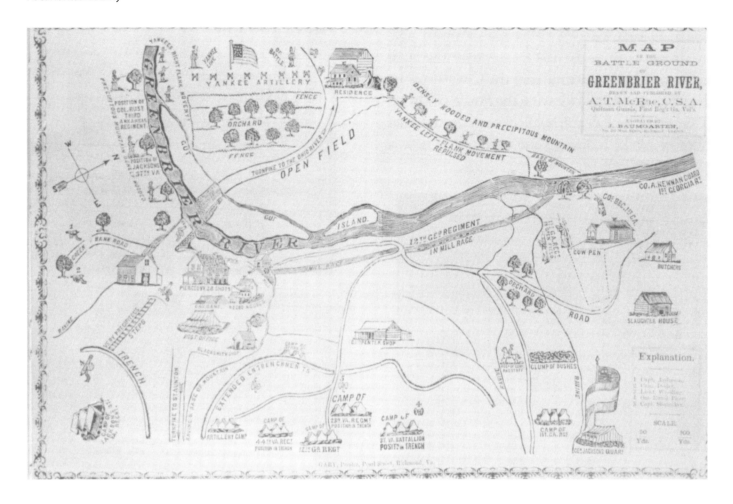

*Huntersville Presbyterian Church**, in Huntersville on state Route 39, four miles east of Marlinton. The town, which was once burned by Federal troops, was the county seat from 1822 to 1891. The church was used as a hospital by both sides. The last battle of the war was supposedly fought here on April 18, 1865, between the 8th Ohio Cavalry and a portion of General W.L. Jackson's army returning to their homes after the surrender.

Joseph Beard Home, on U.S. 219 at the southern edge of Hillsboro. It was built in the 1840s except for the back section which was added sometime after the Civil War. The house was used as a hospital following the Battle of Droop Mountain. Several Confederate soldiers convalesced here for a number of weeks following the battle. It is now a private residence. *Courtesy Bill McNeel*

***Droop Mountain Battlefield State Park**, on U.S. 219 three miles south of Hillsboro. This was the scene of the Battle of Droop Mountain on Nov. 6, 1863 between the Federal forces of Gen. William W. Averell and the Confederate forces of Gen. John Echols. This decisive Federal victory ended serious efforts by the Confederacy to control the new state of West Virginia. The site was purchased by the state in 1928 and dedicated as a state park on July 4, 1929. Much of the original park work was done by the Civilian Conservation Corps.

***Millpoint**, at the junction of U.S. 219 and state Route 39. The existing mill, which operated until 1941, was built right after the Civil War to replace a series of mills dating back to 1778. During the war there was much activity here by both armies because of its strategic location.

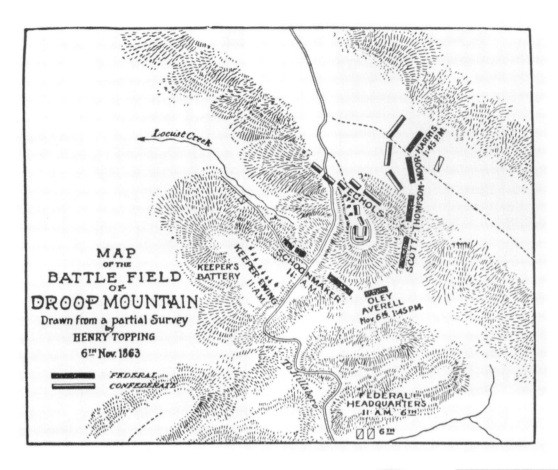

MAP
OF THE
BATTLE FIELD
OF
DROOP MOUNTAIN
Drawn from a partial Survey
by
HENRY TOPPING
6TH Nov. 1863

FEDERAL
CONFEDERATE

Observation tower at Droop Mountain State Park overlooking the beautiful Allegheny Mountains. *SWV*

Monument to John D. Baxter, marking the spot where Baxter, orderly sergeant, Co. F, 10th W.Va. Infantry, fell inside the Confederate line leading the last charge on Nov. 6, 1863. *Courtesy Terry Lowry*

Preston County

Monument to Lieut. Henry Bender.
Courtesy Tim McKinney

A small museum at Droop Mountain State Park.

Tray Run Viaduct, on state Route 72 just north of Rowlesburg on the mainline of the Baltimore & Ohio Railroad at the time of the Civil War. The original viaduct, the largest in the world at the time it was built in 1852, carried the railroad over Tray Run. The pillars were made of large stone blocks, and the tracks crossed a cast iron bridge 600 feet long and 50 feet above the pillars. This was one of the most important sections of the railroad and was heavily guarded by Federal troops throughout the war. The viaduct appears on the obverse side of the Great Seal of the State of West Virginia.

Cheat River Bridge Piers, on U.S. 50 two miles west of Macomber. These piers held up a long covered bridge over Cheat River that was built in 1835. It was a major bridge on the Northwestern Turnpike (present day U.S. 50) and was used by both armies. On April 27, 1863, Confederate Gen. William E. Jones' army passed over the bridge and tore up the decking on one side which took two years to repair. The bridge burned down in 1964.

Putnam County

Battle of Winfield site, sign on courthouse lawn. Just down from the courthouse on Ferry Street is the first ferry site in this area, across the Kanawha River, dating back to 1819. The ferry master's house at the end of the street was built in 1883 but two pre-war tombstones are embedded in the floor. Trenches are reportedly behind the house.

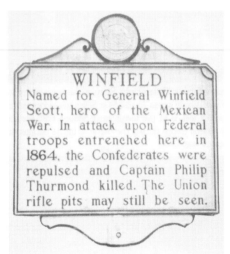

WINFIELD
Named for General Winfield Scott, hero of the Mexican War. In attack upon Federal troops entrenched here in 1864, the Confederates were repulsed and Captain Philip Thurmond killed. The Union rifle pits may still be seen.

Hurricane Bridge Battle site, at the junction of U.S. 60 and state Route 34, just south of Hurricane. This was the scene of a battle on March 28, 1863. The Confederates knew that at Point Pleasant there were quantities of Federal army supplies and a large number of horses. Gen. Albert G. Jenkins, commanding a cavalry brigade at Dublin Depot, on the Virginia and Tennessee Railroad, proposed a raid across the mountains and down the Kanawha Valley to capture the supplies. On March 20 a detachment of 800 men, partly made up of the 8th and 16th Virginia cavalry regiments, commanded by General Jenkins himself, began the 200-mile march over the mountains, despite bad roads and weather.

On March 27 the column reached Hurricane Bridge, where there was a Federal force consisting of Co. A, under Captain Johnson; Co. B, under Capt. Milton Stewart; Co. D, under Capt. Simon Williams; all of the 13th W.Va. Infantry, and Co. G, of the 11th W.Va.

Early in the morning of the 28th, Maj. James Nowling, of the Confederate forces, under a flag of truce, reached the headquarters of Captain Stewart, the senior Federal officer, and demanded an unconditional surrender. Stewart refused to comply, and Major Nowling left, remarking that "within 30 minutes an attack will be made," and he made good his threat. Soon the sound of musketry was heard; fire was returned with much effectiveness, and for five hours the engagement continued. The Confederates then withdrew and resumed their march toward the mouth of the Kanawha. The Federals suffered several casualties, but none were reported by the Confederates.

The site of a Federal fort just above the site of the Hurricane Bridge.

119

*Buffalo Academy, which was built in 1849 in Buffalo on state Route 62. Gen. John McCausland attended the school, and during the war it served as a Confederate barracks and hospital. The site was known as Camp Buffalo in the early days of the 1861 Kanawha Valley Campaign.

*Buffalo Presbyterian Church, adjacent to the Buffalo Academy and undoubtedly used as the Academy was during the war.

The Buffalo Academy as it looked during the war.
Courtesy Emma Simms Maginnis

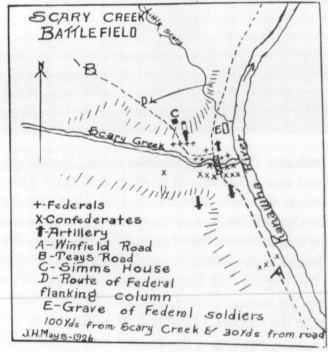

Scary Creek Battlefield Site, at the junction of U.S. 35 and county routes 33 and 44 at Scary, just opposite Nitro. Scary Creek is in the foreground, Simms Hill, occupied by Federal troops during the battle, is in the background.
Courtesy Terry Lowry

Scary Creek Battlefield Site (at left) and current bridge over Scary Creek.

General Cox.

General Wise.

Scary Creek Battlefield Monument, at the bridge across Scary Creek on U.S. 35 at Scary. This monument was erected by the St. Albans Chapter of the United Daughters of the Confederacy to commemorate the battle fought here on July 17, 1861. Confederate Gen. Henry A. Wise won the first southern victory in the Kanawha Valley, but Federal Gen. Jacob D. Cox soon received reinforcements and drove the Confederates up the valley.

Raleigh County

Randolph County

***Wildwood** (Gen. Alfred Beckley House), 117 Laurel Terrace in Beckley. Originally constructed in 1835-36 by Alfred Beckley, the son of a prominent Virginia political figure and first librarian of Congress. Alfred spent 13 years in the United States army prior to the Civil War and was a general in the Confederate army. His endeavors and land donations were a major contribution to the building of the city of Beckley, which is named for him. The village that would become Beckley was besieged and occupied in turn by both armies, although it was shelled only once, by Federal troops in 1863. Future presidents Rutherford B. Hayes and William McKinley were stationed here briefly. General Beckley and other prominent West Virginians, including former governor C.W. Meadows, are buried in Wildwood Cemetery across the highway from the house.

Col. John Augustine Washington Monument, at Elkwater on U.S. 219. Washington, an aide-de-camp to Gen. Robert E. Lee, was killed here on Sept. 13, 1861. He was the last owner of Mount Vernon. The monument was placed here in 1926 by the Randolph Chapter of the United Daughters of the Confederacy.

Valley Mountain Monument, off of U.S. 219 just over the border in Randolph County, north of Mace, Pocahontas County. This was the campsite of General Lee's command in 1861. During "his stay on the mountain, he did not have a beard, only a mustache. But due to the lack of barbers, facilities for shaving and unseasonably cool weather he started growing a beard which would be his trademark throughout the war.

*See/Ward House, (left) on US. Route 219/250, near Mill Creek. This property was the location of a Federal camp and battery during McClellan's Rich Mountain campaign of 1861, as well as the site of some of the action associated with the 1863 Battle of Beverly. It also served as a hospital. The nearby closely associated cemetery, contains the graves of several Confederate soldiers. The house is now a private residence.

*Rich Mountain Battlefield site, five miles west of Beverly on the old Parkersburg and Staunton Turnpike. Scene of an early western Virginia campaign battle on July 11, 1861. This battle was part of Gen. George McClellan's campaign to drive the Confederates from this part of western Virginia. A force of several thousand Confederates under Lt. Col. John Pegram was entrenched on top of Rich Mountain at the Hart farm. Gen. William Rosecrans, leading close to 2,000 Federals, attacked, and in a brief battle routed the Confederates. Federal casualties were fewer than 20 killed and 40 wounded, and the Confederates had more than 100 killed, wounded or captured.

Huttonsville, at the junction of U.S. 219 & 250, 17 miles south of Elkins. The village occupied a prominent position because the principal roads controlling the Tygart Valley River valley forked here. Troops of both sides occupied the village.

Boulders in the battlefield site. Several boulders have inscriptions of wounded soldiers carved upon them.

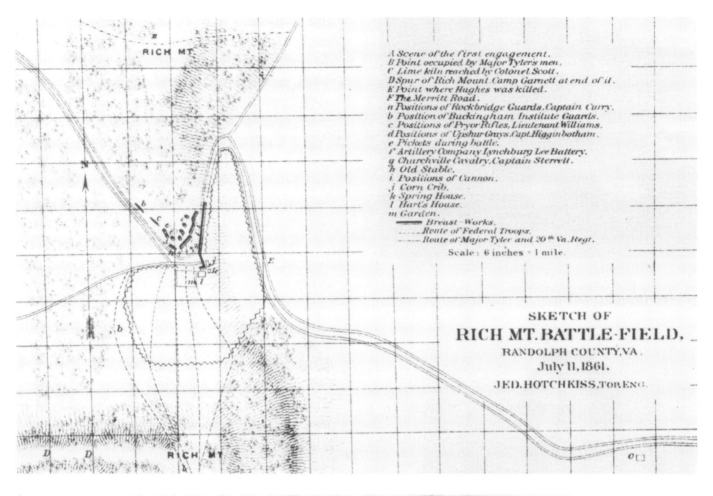

A Scene of the first engagement.
B Point occupied by Major Tyler's men.
C Lime kiln reached by Colonel Scott.
D Spur of Rich Mount. Camp Garnett at end of it.
E Point where Hughes was killed.
F The Merritt Road.
a Positions of Rockbridge Guards, Captain Curry.
b Position of Buckingham Institute Guards.
c Positions of Pryor Rifles, Lieutenant Williams.
d Positions of Upshur Grays, Capt. Higginbotham.
e Pickets during battle.
f Artillery Company Lynchburg Lee Battery.
g Churchville Cavalry, Captain Sterrett.
h Old Stable.
i Positions of Cannon.
j Corn Crib.
k Spring House.
l Hart's House.
m Garden.
▬▬▬ Breast-Works.
-------- Route of Federal Troops.
-·-·-·- Route of Major Tyler and 20th Va. Regt.

Scale: 6 inches = 1 mile.

SKETCH OF
RICH MT. BATTLE-FIELD,
RANDOLPH COUNTY, VA.
July 11, 1861.
JED. HOTCHKISS, Top. Eng.

THE BATTLE OF RICH MOUNTAIN VIRGINIA, JULY 11, 1861.

A July 21, 1861, *Harpers Weekly* engraving of the Rich Mountain Battle.

HART HOUSE

Rich Mountain battle was waged near Hart House and barn where deLagnel's 310 men held Rosecrans' forces for 4 hours before surrendering. This forced Col. Pegram to retreat. His army was captured.

The Hart farm at Rich Mountain looking north from the Federal side, July 1884. The house was used as a hospital after the battle. *WVU*

Gen. George B. McClellan.

*Cheat Mountain Summit, off U.S. 250 on an unimproved dirt road one-and-a-half miles west of Cheat Bridge. More than 4,000 feet above sea level, this was the highest fortified camp maintained by the Federals in the war. It was variously called Fort Milroy, White Top and Camp McClellan.

This site was first occupied by Union troops soon after the withdrawal of Confederate forces to the Greenbrier area in July 1861. General McClellan personally visited the area soon thereafter and rode to the present site of Cheat Bridge which was his farthest personal advance eastward in his western Virginia campaign.

The *Richmond Dispatch* of Sept. 18, 1861, reported that the encampment ". . . is built on the summit of Cheat Mountain . . . just where the road descends on both sides. The forest along the road at this point . . . consists of the white pine, which are tall and stand close together, while the undergrowth is almost wholly mountain laurel, so dense and interlocked as to be almost impenetrable. Here the enemy cleared several acres on each side of the road. On the outer boundary they placed the tall pines they had cut down, partially trimmed and skinned, with their tops outward; presenting to any one approaching a mass of sharp points raised to a considerable height, and strongly interlocked. Inside this they built a wall of logs and cut a deep ditch. In the road they built up, in line with the fortifications, breastworks of great strength and mounted them with pivot guns, while in the center they erected a blockhouse pierced and armed also with cannon. On the east side from the Cheat River, one-and-a-half miles distant, they cleared the road for some distance on both sides, and this can be all the way swept by cannon. The same is the case on the road outwardly for some distance."

Log buildings were later constructed within the breastworks by the first steam sawmill used west of the Alleghenies. These crude buildings were 20-by-40 feet and were provided with a fireplace at one end. Troops of the 32nd Ohio Regiment, with four to six buildings per company, occupied this encampment as winter quarters on Nov. 1, 1861, and, for the most part, abandoned it in April 1862. Remnants of the fortifications can still be seen today.

CHEAT SUMMIT CAMP

Also called Fort Milroy. Fortified camp in gap at the crest of White Top of Cheat Mountain. Occupied by Federal troops during fall and winter of 1861-1862; repulsed threats in Lee's mountain campaign in 1861. Fort's command of the Parkersburg-Staunton Turnpike prevented Lee's army from advancing inland. Above 4,000 feet elevation. highest Union fort in the Civil War.

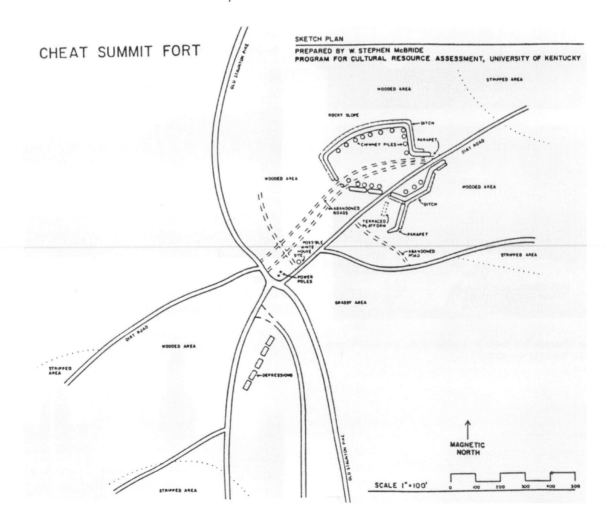

CHEAT SUMMIT FORT

SKETCH PLAN
PREPARED BY W. STEPHEN McBRIDE
PROGRAM FOR CULTURAL RESOURCE ASSESSMENT, UNIVERSITY OF KENTUCKY

SCALE 1" = 100'

MAGNETIC NORTH

Stone fortification remains at the Cheat Summit Fort. *Courtesy Tim McKinney*

Cheat Mountain Fort drawn by a soldier of the 2nd West Virginia Infantry, *Courtesy WVU Archives*

Cheat Mountain Fort remains. Severe strip mining has occurred in the vicinity of the fort.

Beverly Historic Site, five miles south of Elkins on U.S. 219. One of the most important historic sites in the state relating to the Civil War. (Monument in the Beverly Public Square shown.)

Beverly Campground, east of Beverly. These fields were used by Federal forces as a major campsite and staging area during 1863-64. Troops dispatched from these camps participated in numerous campaigns including Droop Mountain. *Courtesy Tim McKinney*

*Beverly Cemetery**, at the north end of Beverly. One of the oldest cemeteries west of the Alleghenies, dating from 1768. Several Confederate soldiers are buried here.

Ward Home and Mt. Iser Cemetery (Butcher Hill Historic District), on a hill, east of and overlooking Beverly. Trenches are still plainly visible around the house (above right). It is now a private residence.

Mt. Iser Cemetery is said to he the only privately owned Confederate Cemetery in the United States. At least 69 Confederate soldiers and one civilian are buried here. The monument was erected in 1908 by the United Daughters of the Confederacy in memory of the men who were killed in the Beverly vicinity. It is located on private property.

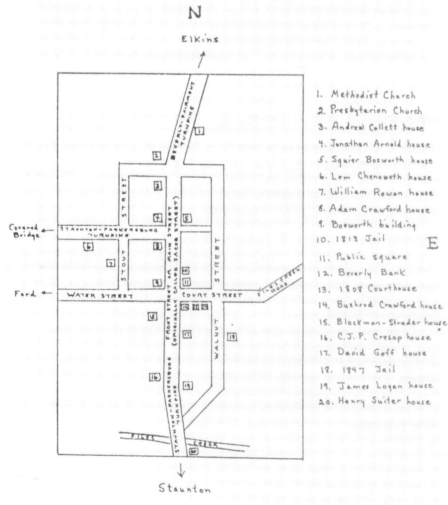

1. Methodist Church
2. Presbyterian Church
3. Andrew Collett house
4. Jonathan Arnold house
5. Squier Bosworth house
6. Lem Chenoweth house
7. William Rowan house
8. Adam Crawford house
9. Bosworth building
10. 1813 Jail
11. Public square
12. Beverly Bank
13. 1808 Courthouse
14. Bushrod Crawford house
15. Blackman-Strader house
16. C.J.P. Cresap house
17. David Goff house
18. 1847 Jail
19. James Logan house
20. Henry Suiter house

*David Goff House, on U.S. 219 in Beverly. This home was built in 1835 by the then prosecuting attorney, David Goff. He later became the first superintendent of schools of Randolph County, having been elected in 1853. On the day of the Battle of Rich Mountain, Colonel Goff together with his family and others, set out upon their journey to the South. He feared that his life would be in danger if he remained, since his sympathies for the South were well known.

When peace was declared, Colonel Goff returned to Beverly to find that his property had been much abused and damaged. The Federals had taken possession of his house and used it as a hospital. Soldiers had carved flags on the walls along with their names, including that of a nurse, Mary Poughkeepsie of McKeesport, Pa. The yard and garden had been used as a burying ground for the amputated limbs of the soldiers.

In the 1920s Randolph Stalnaker renovated the house and added the porch. It has been occupied by several different families, and is now a private residence.

*Adam Crawford Home, on U.S. 219 in Beverly. Mr. Crawford died in 1860, and Mrs. Mary E. Crawford and her family were compelled to live in one room of the house during the Civil War when officers took over the rest of the home for quarters. Tradition says that the first telegraph office to be set up in a permanent structure during the war was erected in a second floor bedroom of this house and that immediately after the Battle of Rich Mountain, the first news of McClellan's victory was sent from that telegraph.

This story gains credence inasmuch as young Harriet Crawford fell in love with a young Union telegrapher. However, she said that she could not marry a Northerner. Mrs. Margaret Scott Phillips then helped the soldier, George Prince, to escape by a secret way over Rich Mountain in order to desert the Union and join the Confederates at Huttonsville. The couple were later married and lived in Beverly, where he was a carpenter. (On the other hand, the helpful Mrs. Phillips' brother felt differently and captured 25 Southern soldiers after the Battle of Rich Mountain, demonstrating once again the divisions that war can cause in families.) The house is now a private residence.

*Blackman-Bosworth Store, on U.S. 219 in Beverly. The brick building known as the S.N. Bosworth Store was built about 1827-28 as one of the first brick buildings to be used for commercial purposes west of the Alleghenies. It was built by slave labor for David Blackman, who was in the mercantile business in Beverly until the beginning of the Civil War. A stone vault in the building was often used as a storage place for valuables before banks came to Randolph County.

This structure has served as a Civil War commissary, a post office, a printing shop, a recreational facility, a general store, and now as the Randolph County Museum. For many years Mr. Blackman's store was the principal one in the county.

*Logan House, (left) located on the left at the bend on South Main Street in Beverly. It was used as a hospital during the war, and it was here that the first Federal amputation was performed. Dr. John Taylor Huff, who had joined the Confederate service, had his headquarters at Philippi. The Federals made a surprise attack on the Confederates, and Dr. Huff lost his kit of instruments and most of his clothing. Two young Confederates were seriously wounded in the attack. Trooper Hanger had his leg shot off by a cannon in Philippi where a Federal surgeon amputated his limb. (The trooper later became famous for making artificial limbs.) The other soldier, Capt. Leroy Parker Daingerfield, was brought to Beverly, a distance of 30 miles from Philippi, needing an amputation. Having lost all his instruments, Dr. Huff had to use a butcher knife to make the skin flap and a tenon saw to sever the bone. The operation was performed on June 4, 1861. The young captain made an uneventful recovery and lived until 1905. The house is now a private residence.

*Bushrod Crawford House. This property was part of the original town Lot #14, one half acre, deeded in 1792 from James Westfall to James Bruff. This house was built about 1850. It was the second house to be used as a telegraph office during the Civil War. In fact, the telegraph office was set up permanently here, probably because General McClellan made his headquarters here. At that time, Bushrod Crawford lived here and was a merchant. The building was used as a tavern. The building is now occupied by the Beverly Heritage Center and the Rich Mountain Battlefield Foundation.

Bushrod Crawford House
Hill Store
Courthouse, 1808

Bank, 1900

*Original County Courthouse and Jail, in Beverly. It was built in 1808 and used until 1894 when a new courthouse was built. After the second courthouse burned, the records were returned to this original building until they were moved to Elkins in 1902. The jail was completed in 1841 and continued in use as the county jail until about 1920 even though the county seat had moved to Elkins in 1902. This complex now houses the Beverly Heritage Center and the Rich Mountain Visitor Center.

*Henry Suiter House, on U.S. 219, on the south end of Beverly. During the war years the little house witnessed many happenings and was in the line of fire during a raid on July 2, 1863. The house was struck, and many exploded shells fell in the yard that day, while the two armies fought to secure Beverly. And in the midst of the noise and destruction, a baby girl was born in the house to Martha Suiter and her husband, Judson. Later, two of the shells were picked up in the yard for the new baby to hand down to her own children as a memento of that birth day. The house is now a private home.

Skirmish at Middlefork Bridge on the Upshur-Randolph County line. Published in *Leslie's Weekly*.

Ritchie County

Gen. Thomas M. Harris Grave, in the Odd Fellows Cemetery in Harrisville. Harris was born in 1817 and was named after his grandfather. He spent most of the pre-Civil War years in Parkersburg, Glenville and Harrisville. He became a doctor in 1843 and at the outbreak of the war organized the 10th West Virginia Regiment. His service was mostly in West Virginia and the Shenandoah Valley. He obtained the rank of major general during the 1865 Petersburg campaign. He served on the commission that tried the Lincoln conspirators and left the army in 1866. He served in the state legislature, was state Adjutant General, a pension agent in Wheeling and continued to practice medicine. He died in Harrisville in 1906. *Courtesy Joe Ferrell*

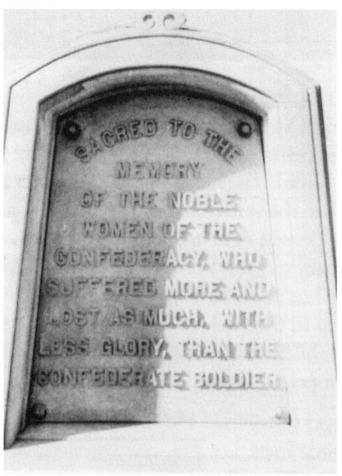

Confederate Monument, First and James streets in Hinton. A 15-foot metal statue of a Confederate soldier mounted on a granite base, in the center of a small triangular park. Erected in 1914, the monument bears an embossed likeness of Gen. Robert E. Lee, and commemorates the Confederate soldiers of the Greenbrier and New River valleys.

Mike Foster Monument, in the Forest Hill Cemetery, Hinton. A 10-foot shaft of white marble erected in 1907, commemorates Foster, a Confederate soldier from the New River Valley, whose bravery under fire was legendary in this region.

Taylor County

Pruntytown Jail, at the junction of U.S. 50 and 250 in Pruntytown just west of Grafton. This handmade brick structure was built around 1844. The first slaves in the country freed by the order of President Lincoln on Nov. 22, 1862, were released from this jail, where they had been confined by their masters who feared they intended to run away and join the Federal troops. The president declared these slaves "contraband of war" and issued orders to General B.F. Butler for their release. Butler wired the order to Brig. Gen. Robert H. Milroy who commanded the Cheat Mountain Division. Milroy in turn wired Lt. Ephraim Chalfant in command of Light Battery D at Grafton who set them free.

*Webster, on U.S. 119/250 just south of Grafton. This was a huge Federal supply depot early in the war supplying troops in the Belington, Beverly and Cheat Mountain areas. This Civil War era house was the birthplace in 1864 of Anna M. Jarvis, the founder of Mother's Day.

Covered Bridge Pier, in the Tygart Valley River near U.S. 50 at Grafton. These piers are all that remain of a covered bridge built in 1834-35 on the Northwestern Turnpike. It was used by both sides during the war and destroyed by a flood in 1888.

*Grafton National Cemetery, 431 Walnut Street in Grafton. It was established by the Federal government in 1868 for the interment of Civil War dead. There are 1,200 Federal and Confederate soldiers buried here and more than 4,000 total war dead buried in three terraces. Thornsberry Bailey Brown is also interred here.

Thornsberry Bailey Brown Monument, on U.S. 50 just west of the bridge over the Tygart Valley River at Grafton. The first Federal soldier fatality of the Civil War, Pvt. Thornsberry Bailey Brown, was killed at Fetterman (now Grafton).

On the night of May 22, 1861, Lt. Daniel Wilson and Private Brown were ordered to Fetterman to inspect the force and position of the enemy. At the point where the tracks of the Baltimore and Ohio Railroad crossed the Northwestern Turnpike, Lieutenant Wilson encountered the enemy's pickets, who called him to halt. Lieutenant Wilson ordered Private Brown to fire on the enemy, and Brown's shot nicked one of the pickets in the ear. A moment later Brown fell mortally wounded with three breast wounds. Thus he was the first enlisted soldier in the United States to give up his life in the Civil War to an organized force of Confederates.

A monument to his memory was erected at the point where Brown lost his life, by the Betsy Ross Tent No. 10, Daughters of Union Veterans, on May 22, 1928. The monument was later moved to its present location. The original base of the monument is still located on the spot where he was shot, by the side of the railroad tracks, about one half mile distant.

Private Brown was first interred in a cemetery near Remington. In 1903, the Grand Army of the Republic of Grafton was granted permission by his relatives to exhume his remains and the body was brought to Grafton and interred in the National Cemetery.

Wilson and Brown were members of the so called "Grafton Guards" who became Company B of the Second West Virginia Infantry Volunteers. The Confederate pickets were members of Letcher's Guards.

Inscription on T. Bailey Brown Monument Grafton National Cemetery, Grafton, W.Va.
MAY 15, 1829-MAY 22, 1861 DEDICATED
by Reno Post No. 7 G.A.R.
in Memory of
T. Bailey Brown of Co. B.
2nd W.Va. Vol. Inft. Capt.
George R. Latham, Comdg.
The First Union Soldier
Killed in the Civil War at
Fetterman, W.Va., May 22,
1861 by Daniel Knight of
Co. A 25th Va. C.S.A. Capt.
John A. Robinson, Comdg.
"Grafton, W.Va., Jan. 23, 1865. I certify that Thonsbury [sic] B. Brown was enrolled in Co. B., 2d Va. Vols. Inf. at Grafton, "W.Va. (then Va.) on the 15th day of May, 1861, and rendezvoused with said company at said place preparatory to muster into the U.S. Service, until the evening of May 23, 1861 [he was off by one day), when he was shot while in line of duty by the picket of the Rebels at Fetterman, and almost instantly killed. The Company was mustered in on May 25, 1861, but said Brown's name was necessarily not borne on the roll."
"Signed, George R. Latham, Colonel, 6th W.Va. Cavalry, Late Co. B, 2d Va. Vol. Inf."

West Main Street Methodist Church, on West Main Street in Grafton. This part of Grafton was known as Fetterman during the Civil War. In July 1861 the Federal government took possession of the Methodist Episcopal Church at Fetterman and established the first temporary hospital in the county for the treatment of ill and wounded troops. It was used until a large permanent hospital was opened in February 1862 in West Grafton. The church was then used to quarter Federal troops. In 1915 the church received $490 from the United States government for damage done during the war.

Tucker County

Gen. Robert S. Garnett

BATTLE OF CARRICK'S FORD, WESTERN VIRGINIA—DISCOVERY OF THE BODY OF GENERAL GARNETT, BY MAJOR GORDON AND COLONEL DUMONT, AFTER THE BATTLE.

Corrick's Ford, on U.S. 219 just west of Parsons. This ford across Shavers Fork was the scene of the Battle of Corrick's Ford on July 13, 1861. Brig. Gen. Robert Selden Garnett, killed here, was the first Confederate general to be killed in the war. Seventy-seven Confederate and 51 Federal generals would be killed in the four year conflict. Garnett was taken to the nearby home of William Corrick where he died a short time later. This battle was a continuation of the Rich Mountain conflict and the Confederate rearguard action at the ford was not successful and most of their wagon train was lost.

Corricks Ford monument at the Tucker County Courthouse, Parsons.

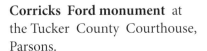

Upshur County

Upshur Militia, at the junction of state Routes 4 and 20 at Rock Cave in the southern part of the county.

Wayne County

*Z.D. Ramsdell House**, 1108-B Street, Ceredo. It was built by Z.D. Ramsdell in 1858 as the first brick house in Ceredo, just one year following the founding of the community by Eli Thayer. Ramsdell was a bootmaker and staunch abolitionist who endorsed and supported Eli Thayer's philosophy that steam power could replace slave power in developing industry. He was a captain in the Federal army. The house is now a museum owned by the Ceredo Historic Landmark Commission.

Webster County

Perry Connolly Grave, one mile south of Cowen, and then two-tenths of a mile on the John Goff Road. He was the commander of the Moccasin Rangers, a Confederate guerrilla unit that operated in the northern and eastern regions of West Virginia. One of their favorite targets was the Baltimore and Ohio Railroad line in northern West Virginia. Connolly was Nancy Hart's lover and died in action on Jan. 2, 1862. *Courtesy Ron Hardway, Upper Glade*

Wirt County

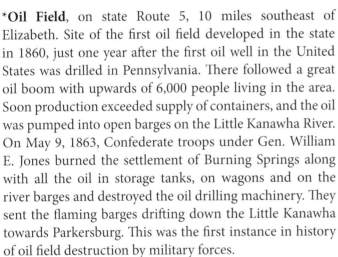

*Oil Field, on state Route 5, 10 miles southeast of Elizabeth. Site of the first oil field developed in the state in 1860, just one year after the first oil well in the United States was drilled in Pennsylvania. There followed a great oil boom with upwards of 6,000 people living in the area. Soon production exceeded supply of containers, and the oil was pumped into open barges on the Little Kanawha River. On May 9, 1863, Confederate troops under Gen. William E. Jones burned the settlement of Burning Springs along with all the oil in storage tanks, on wagons and on the river barges and destroyed the oil drilling machinery. They sent the flaming barges drifting down the Little Kanawha towards Parkersburg. This was the first instance in history of oil field destruction by military forces.

Wood County

City Park Cannon, located in the Parkersburg City Park. This cannon was not at Fort Boreman during the war but was placed at the fort site in the early 1890s when Captains Kirk and Shaw of the local GAR post urged the placement as a memorial to their fallen comrades. The cannon was sent from Pittsburgh and was fired on holidays and other occasions until 1920 when someone tampered with it to prevent its ever being fired again. It was then sold to a junkyard, but the Parkersburg Kiwanis Club salvaged it and placed it on a plot donated by the city in City Park. A concrete carriage was built for the gun.

* **Parkersburg General Hospital**, on the northeast corner of Fourth and Avery streets in Parkersburg. This house, owned by Henry Logan, served as a major Federal hospital until June 13, 1865. *Courtesy Trans Allegheny Books*

Confederate Memorial, in the City Park, Parkersburg. The Wood County Confederate Monument Association erected this 23-ton monument with a seven-foot bronze figure of a Confederate soldier in 1908. The bronze plaque on the front states:

CONFEDERATE STATES OF AMERICA
DEO VINDICE
FEB. 22, 1862
IN MEMORY OF OUR CONFEDERATE DEAD
ERECTED BY PARKERSBURG CHARTER UDC 1908

View of Parkersburg from the south side of the Little Kanawha River where it joins the Ohio. By John H.B. Latrobe, from *Notices of Parkersburg, Virginia,* as it is in July, 1860. *Courtesy Blennerhassett Historical Park Commission*

Coleman Chapel, south of Belleville. The chapel was built in 1860 as a Methodist Episcopal Church South. During the war it was used as a barracks and headquarters for local loyal militia and home guards and at times as an outpost by (Federal) Captain Loysdons Wood County Militia. *Courtesy Trans Allegheny Books*

*****Fort Boreman Hill**, overlooking Parkersburg from across the Little Kanawha River. The fort was built in the summer and fall of 1863 to protect the Baltimore and Ohio Railroad terminal. It was originally called Fort Logan (on Mount Logan) but later was named Fort Boreman for Wood County native, Arthur I. Boreman, first governor of West Virginia. It was defended by 136 men, but there was never a shot fired against the enemy from the fort.

Site of Fort Boreman in 1897 with faint outlines of trenches. *Courtesy Trans Allegheny Books*

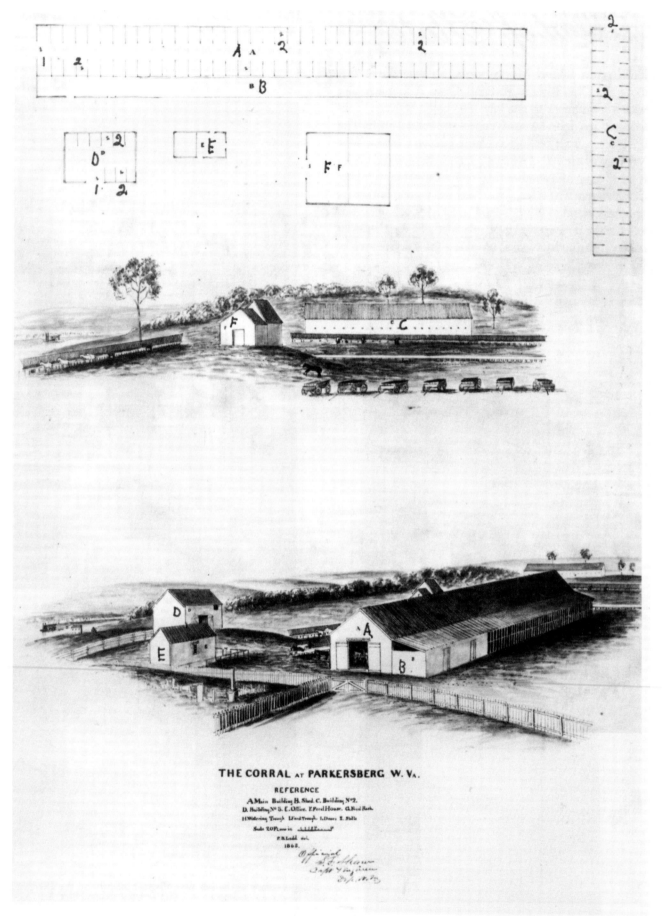

THE CORRAL AT PARKERSBERG W. VA.

REFERENCE

A. Main Building B. Shed C. Building No 2.
D. Building No 3. E. Office. F. Feed House. G. Rest Rack.
H. Watering Trough I. Feed Trough J. Doors K. Stalls

Scale 20 Feet to 1 Inch

F. R. Ladd del.
1865.

Wyoming County

Confederate Grave, in the Hiram Clay Cemetery in Pineville, Wyoming County, at the intersection of state Route 10 and Bear Hole Road. Hiram Clay (1840- 1896) was a private in Company G, 22nd Virginia Infantry. In 1990 the tombstone was dedicated, the first such dedication in the county in years. Clay's grandson and granddaughter were in attendance along with the American Legion and Civil War reenactors (Hal Walls is pictured). *Courtesy Shelley Clay Hill, Lester, W.Va.*

Buffington Island Monuments, on state Route 124, along the Ohio River at Portland, Ohio. A four-acre plot with a monument to the July 1863 battle between Confederate Gen. John Morgan's raiders and Federal forces. The site is across from Buffington Island, Jackson County, West Virginia, where 700 of Morgan's men were captured on July 19. Morgan and another 1,200 men escaped but were later captured near West Point, Ohio. Near this monument stands another erected to honor Maj. Daniel McCook, who was killed in the Buffington Island battle. McCook was the leader of the "Fighting McCooks" his nine sons and five sons of his brother, Dr. John McCook.

Traveller's Grave, on the grounds of Washington and Lee University in Lexington, Virginia, near the Lee Chapel. This is the grave of Gen. Robert E. Lee's horse, Traveller, which he obtained in Fayette County, West Virginia, in 1861. *Courtesy Tim McKinney*

Monument to the 7th West Virginia Infantry on the Gettysburg Battlefield. Erected by the state of West Virginia and dedicated on Sept. 28, 1898. *W.VA. Dept. of Culture & History*

Belle Boyd Gravesite in Wisconsin Dells, Wis. She was born in Martinsburg, Berkeley County, in 1844 and died June 12, 1900, in Wisconsin, *Martinsburg Public Library*

A monument to Confederate Col. George S. Patton, from Kanawha County, stands in the Stonewall Confederate Cemetery at Mt. Hebron Cemetery in Winchester, Virginia. Patton formed the famed "Kanawha Riflemen" in Charleston, West Virginia which became part of the 22nd Virginia Infantry Regiment. He fought at Scary Creek, White Sulphur Springs and Droop Mountain and was killed at the Battle of Winchester on September 19, 1864.

A monument honoring Maj. Gen. Jesse Reno, a West Virginia native, was rededicated on Sept. 16, 1989 at Fox's Gap, South Mountain, Maryland. The monument was placed there 100 years earlier. Reno was killed at the action at Fox's Gap on Sept. 14, 1862. He was born in Wheeling in 1823 and was graduated eighth in his West Point class of 1846, earning brevets of first lieutenant and captain in the Mexican War. He commanded a brigade in Ambrose Burnside's North Carolina expedition in the winter of 1861-62. The bearded Reno, who stood about 5 feet 5 inches, was described by Orlando Willcox, a division commander in the IX Corps, as an unassuming, enthusiastic, "cold but not phlegmatic" leader. He was shot at Fox's Gap as he rode along his command's lines, encouraging his men. He was buried in Boston on Sept. 20, 1862, his casket covered by a homemade flag given him by Barbara Fritchie when his corps passed through Frederick. In 1867 his remains were taken to Georgetown, DC. and reinterred in Oak Hill Cemetery. *Courtesy Lt. Col. William McConnell.*

This cannon, called the **Lewisburg Gun,** was captured from the Confederates by members of the 44th Ohio Volunteer Infantry at the Battle of Lewisburg on May 22, 1862. At the time of this photo it stood in front of the Veterans Memorial Hall in Springfield, Ohio. It is now stored inside the building and owned by the Clark County Historical Society. *W.VA. Dept. of Culture & History*

Monument to the 4th West Virginia Infantry at the Vicksburg National Military Park in Mississippi. The bust is of Maj. Arza Goodspeed, killed at Vicksburg. *W.VA. Dept. of Culture & History*

Appendix

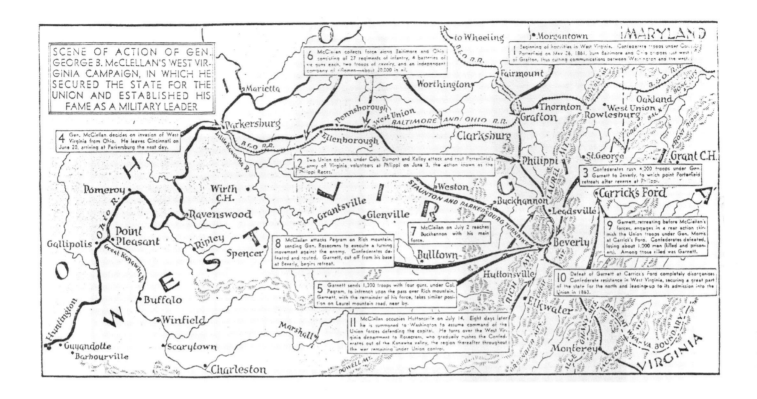

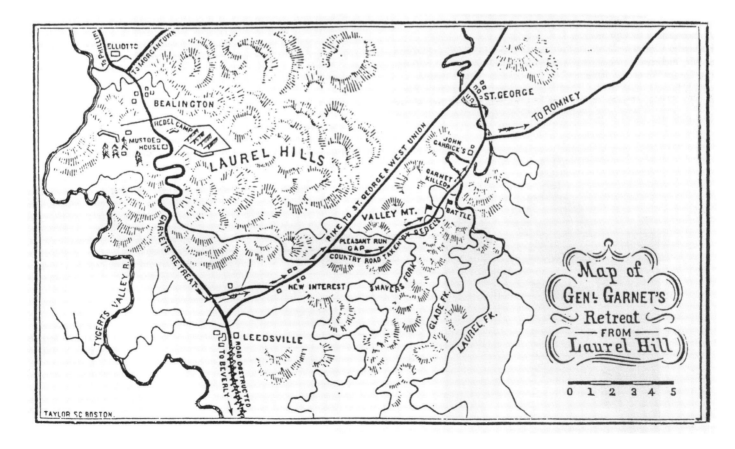

General muster of militia at a West Virginia county seat before the Civil War, required to be held at least once each year. No uniforms were provided and few were owned and worn. Officers were distinguished by colored sashes and each man provided his own arms. Because of the division in the ranks, these county militia regiments were of little use in the Civil War. Sketch by Joseph H. Diss Debar. *W. VA. Dept. of Culture & History*

Co. G, Seventh West Virginia Cavalry, copied from an old tintype. Officers:
Capt. James S. Cassady, Fayette County; 1st Lieut. James D. Fellers, 2nd Lieut.
John E. Swaar. The company was recruited in Fayette and Kanawha counties and
immediate area. *W.VA. Dept. of Culture & History*

Col. John H. Oley (later Brevet Brigadier General), and field and staff officers of the Seventh West Virginia Cavalry (formerly the Eighth West Virginia Mounted Infantry). Picture made in 1864, probably at Charleston. *W.VA. Dept. of Culture & History*

Civil War service medals presented to Union soldiers from West Virginia. *W.VA. Dept. of Culture & History*

General Officers of the Civil War from West Virginia

Confederate General Officers
Lt. Gen. Thomas J. "Stonewall" Jackson of Lewis County
Brig. Gen. Albert Gallatin Jenkins of Cabell County
Brig. Gen. John McCausland of Mason County
Brig. Gen. Edwin Lee of Jefferson County*
Brig. Gen. William L. "Mudwall" Jackson of Lewis County*
Brig. Gen. Brickett D. Fry of Kanawha County
Brig. Gen. John Echols of Monroe County
Brig. Gen. John B. Floyd of Monroe County*

Union General Officers
Maj. Gen. Jesse Reno of Ohio County
Maj. Gen. Joseph A.J. Lightburn of Lewis County*
Maj. Gen. Thomas M. Harris of Ritchie County
Maj. Gen. Benjamin Kelley of Ohio County*
Brig. Gen. Isaac H. Duval of Brooke County
Brig. Gen. Nathan Goff Jr. of Harrison County**
Brig. Gen. David Hunter Strother of Morgan County**

*Not born in West Virginia
**Brevet Brig. Gen.

LIEUTENANT-GENERAL THOMAS JONATHAN JACKSON.

General William L. Jackson

General W.W. Loring

General David Hunter Strother

General William W. Averell

Francis H. Pierpont

Arthur I. Boreman

West Virginia—Buried Civil War Congressional Medal of Honor Recipients

NAME	PLACE OF INTERNMENT	CITATION
James F. Adams Pvt. Co. D, 1st WV Cav.	Huntington-Oaklawn	Captured 14th VA Cav flag at Nineveh, VA 11/12/64
Richard Bowry(*) Sgt. Co. C, 1st WV Cav.	Parkersburg	Captured flag at Charlottesville, VA 3/5/65
Hiram R. Howard Pvt. Co. H, 11th OH	Pt. Pleasant	Scaled enemy works & captured flag in hand-to-hand fight at Missionary Ridge, TN 11/25/63
Joseph Kimball Pvt. Co. B, 2nd WV	Alma (Centerville)— Beechwood	Captured 6th NC Inf. flag at Sailor's (Sayler's) Ck. 4/6/65
Walter F. McWhorter Sgt. Co. E, 3rd WV Cav.	Nina (Salem)	Captured 6th TN Inf. flag at Sailor's (Sayler's) Ck. 4/6/65
Charles A. Reeder Pvt. Co. G, 12th WV Inf.	Shinnston	Capture of flag at Battery Gregg (Petersburg) 4/2/65
Levi Shoemaker Sgt. Co. A, 1st WV Cav.	Morgantown	Captured 22nd VA Cav. flag at Nineveh, VA 11/12/64
James C. Summers Pvt. Co. H, 4th WV Inf.	Elkview-Reynolds	Gallantry in charge of the "volunteer storming party" at Vicksburg, MS 5/22/63
Adam White Cpl. Co. K, 1st VA(?) Cav.	Wadeville	Captured flag at Hatcher's Run, VA 4/2/65
Daniel A. Woods Pvt. Co. K, 1st VA(?) Cav.	Wheeling	Captured 18th FLA Inf. flag at Sailor's (Sayler's) Ck. 4/6/65

(*) also listed as Boury.
List researched and compiled by Joseph H. Ferrell & Gary W. Gibson

The Dying Soldier's Lament on the Battlefield

My day of life is over, And here I lay me down In the hot, red
field of battle, In the arms of high renown.
By the shaft of death I'm stricken In my upward flight to fame,
And I give my life to nothingness To win a warrior's name.

—Written by Col. John W. Lowe, 12th Ohio Vol. Infantry,
shortly before his death at the Battle of Carnifex Ferry.

No. *14.5.5.*

Union, Va., January 1st, 1863.

15 ~The County of Monroe~ 15

Will pay to bearer **FIFTEEN CTS.** redeemable in current funds, when presented in five dollars, or its multiple, at the Clerk's office of the said county.

By order of the Court. G. _____ CLERK.

STATE OF VIRGINIA.

25 CENTS. ISSUED BY AN ACT OF THE CORPORATION, OF APRIL 30TH, 1851. **25** CENTS.

Charlestown, *Oct 11* 1861. C.

No. *2137*

DUE BY

THE CORPORATION OF CHARLESTOWN,

TWENTY FIVE CENTS,

Payable in Virginia Bank Notes by _____ *Treasurer,*
to the Bearer, on presentation of these Bills in sums of FIVE DOLLARS.

_____ Clerk of the Board. _____ President.

25 CENTS. **25** CENTS.

Lewisburg, Va., Sept. 1st, 1862.

No. ____

~The County of Greenbrier~

WILL PAY TO BEARER

75 **SEVENTY FIVE CENTS,** **75**

According to Act of Assembly of Virginia, passed March 29, 1862.

_____ Clerk.

____ order of the County Court.

75

FRANKFORD, VA.,

February *9* 1862.

DUE TO BEARER

SEVENTY-FIVE CENTS,

Payable when presented in sums of Ten Dollars.

VIRGINIAN PR. LYNCHBURG _____ _____

75 CTS.

Bibliography

Barten, Thomas H., *Autobiography, Including a History of the Fourth Regiment, West Virginia Volunteers*, Charleston, West Virginia Print Co., 1890.

Boehm, Robert B., *The Civil War in Western Virginia: The Decisive Campaigns of 1861*, Columbus, Ohio State University (Thesis, Ph.D.), 1957.

Branham, James, *Arbitrary Arrest in West Virginia, 1861-1865*, Morgantown, West Virginia University, 1959.

Bright, Simeon M., *The McNeill Rangers: A Study in Confederate Guerrilla Warfare*, Charleston, West Virginia History, Vol. XII, No. 4, 1951.

Brown, Genevieve, *A History of the Sixth Regiment West Virginia Infantry Volunteers*, Charleston, West Virginia History, Vol. IX, No. 4, 1948.

Carnes, Eva M., *The Tygarts Valley Line, June-July 1861*, Philippi, Centennial Commemoration, Inc., 1961.

Cohen, Stan, *The Civil War in West Virginia: A Pictorial History*, Charleston, Pictorial Histories Publishing Co., Inc., 1976.

"Confederate Soldiers of West Virginia," West Virginia Department of Archives and History, Biennial Report, 1931-1933.

The Confederate Veteran Magazine, Nashville, Tenn., Volumes Referencing West Virginia: Vol's II; V-XVI; XIX-XXII; XXIV-XXVI; XXVIII-XL, 1892-1932.

Cook, Bird, "Battlefields of West Virginia" Charleston, West Virginia Bluebook, No. 18, 1934.

Cox, Jacob D., *Military Reminiscences of the Civil War*, New York, Charles Surbrens, 1900.

Curry, Richard O., & F. Gerald Ham, "The Bushwhackers' War: Insurgency and Counter-Insurgency in West Virginia," Columbus, Ohio, *Blue & Gray Magazine*, Vol. II, No. 4, March 1985.

Dickinson, Jack L, *Jenkins of Greenbottom: A Civil War Saga*, Charleston, Pictorial Histories Publishing Co., Inc., 1988.

_____, *16th Virginia Cavalry*, Lynchburg, Va., H.E. Howard, Inc., 1989.

Engle, Stephen Douglas, *Thunder in the Hills; A History of the Civil War in Jefferson County, West Virginia*, Charleston, Mountain State Press, 1989.

Gilbert, Dave, *A Walkers Guide to Harpers Ferry, West Virginia*, Charleston, Pictorial Histories Publishing Co., Inc., 1983.

"Greenbrier in the Civil War" *Journal of the Greenbrier Historical Society*, Lewisburg, Vol. 1, No. 6, 1968.

Hall, Granville D, Lees *Invasion of Northwest Virginia in 1861*, Chicago, Mayer & Miller Co., 1911.

Haselberger, Francis, *Yanks From the South! First Land Campaign of the Civil War*, Baltimore, Md., 1989.

Hewitt, William, *History of the Twelfth West Virginia Volunteer Infantry*, Twelfth W.Va. Infantry Assoc, 1892.

Hite, Delmer R., *Roster of Jackson County, West Virginia Civil War Soldiers*, Murraysville, Jackson Co. Hist. Soc., 1974.

Hornbeck, Betty, *Upshur Brothers of the Blue and the Gray*, Parsons, McClain Printing Co., 1967.

Jones, Allen W., "Military Events in West Virginia During the Civil War, 1861-1865" Charleston, *West Virginia History*, Vol. XXI, No. 3, 1960.

Kincaid, Mary E., "Fayetteville, West Virginia During the Civil War," Charleston, *West Virginia History*, Vol. XIV, No. 4, 1953.

Lang, Theodore E, *Loyal West Virginia from 1861 to 1865*, Baltimore, Deutsch Pub. Co., 1895.

Lowry, Terry, *The Battle of Scary Creek: Military Operations in the Kanawha Valley, April-July, 1861*, Charleston, Pictorial Histories Publishing Co., Inc., 1982.

_____, *22nd Virginia Infantry Regiment*, Lynchburg, Va., H.E. Howard, Inc., 1989.

Lynch, Leona, *Monroe County, West Virginia in the Civil War*, Morgantown, West Virginia University, (M.A. Thesis), 1950.

Matheny, H.E., *Major General Thomas Maley Harris, and Roster of the 10th W.Va. Volunteer Infantry 1861-1865*, Parsons, McClain Printing Co., 1963.

Moore, George E., *A Banner in the Hills; West Virginia Statehood*, New York, Appleton-Century-Crofts, 1963.

McKinney, Tim, *The Civil War in Fayette County, West Virginia*, Charleston, Pictorial Histories Publishing Co., Inc., 1988.

O'Brien, Katherine, *The Seventh West Virginia Volunteer Infantry 1861-1865*, Morgantown (M.A. Thesis) West Virginia University, 1965.

Official Records of the War of the Rebellion of the Union and Confederate Armies, Washington, DC, U.S. Government Printing Office, 1901.

Pauley, Michael J., "They Called Him Tiger John: The Story of General John McCausland, OS. A." Columbus, *Blue & Gray Magazine*, Vol. I, No. 4, 1984.

Powell, William S., "Beginning of the Civil War in West Virginia," Charleston, *West Virginia Review*, Vol. XIV, No. 6, 1937.

Rawling, C.J., *History of the First (West) Virginia Infantry Regiment*, Philadelphia, J.B. Lippincott, 1887.

Reader, Frank S., *History of the Fifth West Virginia Cavalry and of Battery G, First West Virginia Light Artillery*, New Brighton, Penn., ES. Reader, 1890.

Richardson, Hila A., "Raleigh County, West Virginia in the Civil War," Charleston, *West Virginia History*, Vol. X, No. 3, 1949.

Scott, J.L.,*36th Virginia Infantry*, Lynchburg, Va., H.E. Howard, Inc., 1987.